The

CAREER
COACH

Carol Kleiman's

Inside Tips to

Getting *and Keeping*

the Job You Want

Carol Kleiman

 Dearborn
Financial Publishing, Inc.

While a great deal of care has been taken to provide accurate and current information, the ideas, suggestions, general principles and conclusions presented in this text are subject to local, state and federal laws and regulations, court cases and any revisions of same. The reader is thus urged to consult legal counsel regarding any points of law—this publication should not be used as a substitute for competent legal advice.

Publisher: Kathleen A. Welton
Managing Editor: Jack L. Kiburz
Associate Editor: Karen A. Christensen
Editorial Assistant: Stephanie Schmidt
Interior Design: Lucy Jenkins
Cover Design: S. Laird Jenkins Corporation
Author Photo: © Catharine E. Bell

Library of Congress Cataloging-in-Publication Data

Kleiman, Carol.
    The career coach : Carol Kleiman's inside tips to getting and keeping the job you want / by Carol Kleiman.
        p.   cm.
    Includes bibliographical references and index.
    ISBN 0-7931-1088-2 (pbk.)
    1. Job hunting.   2. Vocational guidance.   I. Title.
HF5382.7.K55   1994
650.14—dc20   94-3615
                                                                    CIP

"The Career Coach is loaded with practical, up-to-date career advice—just what we've come to expect from Carol Kleiman. A great resource for career strategists at every level of employment. Don't miss it!"

> Anne Ladky
> Executive Director, Women Employed

"Carol Kleiman shows you how to expertly navigate the ups and downs of your career—and come out on top. Use *The Career Coach* to steer your own course. Smooth sailing!"

> Marilyn Moats Kennedy
> Managing Partner, Career Strategies

"Finding a job has never been tougher. But now, thanks to Carol Kleiman, it's possible to get an edge on the competition, giving you a better chance at winning the game."

> Herb Greenberg
> Syndicated Columnist, *San Francisco Chronicle*

"No one gives better advice about the world of work than Carol Kleiman. She offers up savvy insider-tips and practical advice, in a witty conversational manner that's fun to read. For people just starting out, looking to improve their prospects or make a job change, *The Career Coach* is a user-friendly, invaluable guide."

> Marcia Ann Gillespie
> Editor-in-Chief, *Ms.* magazine

"Nearly everyone can benefit from *The Career Coach*—whether you're looking for a job or just trying to manage your career. I heartily recommend it."

> Jack Erdlen
> Executive Director
> Northeast Human Resources Association

"The Career Coach is an invaluable career handbook for today's restructuring job market. And Kleiman's expert advice is as accessible as a conversation with an insightful friend—one who is savvy, pragmatic and exceptionally plugged in."

> Susan McHenry
> Senior Editor, *Working Woman*

OTHER BOOKS
by Carol Kleiman

You Can Teach Your Child Tennis

Women's Networks:
The Complete Guide to Getting a Better Job,
Advancing Your Career and Feeling Great as a Woman
Through Networking

Killer Tennis
(with John R. Powers)

Speaking of Sex: Mothers and Daughters
(with Catharine E. Kleiman)

The 100 Best Job$ for the 1990s & Beyond

....

DEDICATION

To my daughter, Catharine E. Bell, and my son-in-law, Kevin Bell; to my son, Raymond Kleiman, Jr., and my daughter-in-law, Mary Jane Kleiman; and to my son, Robert Kleiman.

And to the next generation, my grandson, Raymond Mauka Kleiman, 3d, born July 4, 1994.

With thanks for all your love, support and *coaching*.

CONTENTS

Acknowledgments   xi

Preface   xiii

····· **PART ONE** ·····

How To Find a Top Job That's Right for You

1. What Is the *Right* Job?   3

2. Preparing To Find a Job—Kicking Your Resume
    Dependency   15

3. Doing Your Homework—What Really Pays Off   27

4. Landing the Job   39

5. The Job Offer   57

····· **PART TWO** ·····

Keeping Your Job

6. Keeping Current   71

7. First Shoot All the Managers   83

8. Dealing with the Big, Bad Boss   97

9. Organizing Your Job To Succeed   111

10. Letting People Know What You Want   125

····· **PART THREE** ·····

Taking Charge of Your Career

11. Only *You* Care about Your Career   141

12. What To Do if You're Fired   153

13. Networking Every Possible Connection   165

14. Your Own Continuing Education Program   179

15. Your Happiness Quotient   191

····· **PART FOUR** ·····

Helping Others Along the Way— And Yourself

16. How and Why To Help   205

17. Preparing Yourself for a Second Career   217

Appendix A: Where To Go for More Information   231

Appendix B: The 100 Best Jobs and Their Salaries   235

Index   241

ACKNOWLEDGMENTS

Writing a book is a challenging experience—even this, my sixth book—because it is something that ultimately the author must do alone. But I have been extremely fortunate to be surrounded by people who not only encouraged me to write this book but also made it possible by cheering for me along the way. So many people gave me their insights and helped me with their professionalism and kindness that it is impossible to list all their names. But I especially want to thank the following friends and colleagues who are the "yea" sayers: Casey Bell, Jeff Bierig, Terry Brown, Tom Cekay, Dick Ciccone, Bobbi Clark, Jackie Combs, Nadia Cowen, Liz Crown, Pam Cytrynbaum, Jean Davidson, Margo Davis, Bruce DuMont, Terry Fencl, Jack Fuller, Sondra Gair, Melita Marie Garza, Lesley Geary, Lois Gerber, Marcia Ann Gillespie, Sherry Goodman, Mary Ellen Hendricks, Gloria Hochman, Margaret Holt, Bob Howe, Joe Leonard, Grace Kaminowitz, Bob Kahn, Sheila King, Bruce Kramer, Rick Kogan, Anne Ladky, Sherren Leigh, Marion Lezak, Victor Lindquist, Jerome McDonald, Marilyn Miller, Barry Nemcoff, Karen Olson, Judy Peres, Sally Peterson, Joe Petrocik, Wally Phillips, Karen Rew, John Schmeltzer, John Sibbald, Walter Simmons, Al Smedley, Diann Smith, Sandy Spikes, Paul Spindler, Karen Springen, Stacey Steig, Jon Steinberg, Gloria Steinem, Darlene Gavron Stevens, Charles Storch, Al Sutton, Larry Townsend, Howard Tyner, Fran

Victor, Tommy Whitman, Pat Widder, Tony Wilkins, Reshma Memon Yaqub and Owen Youngman.

I also am deeply grateful to Teresa Cavanaugh of Jean Naggar Literary Agency for her kind intelligence and patience, and to Beryl Zitch of Contemporary Forum for her professionalism and support.

Yet again I am awed by the expertise and efficiency of my publisher, Kathleen A. Welton, who dubbed me "The Career Coach" and believed I actually could learn to use a new computer; by Irmgard Cooper, who actually taught me to use it; and of Bobbye Middendorf, Dearborn's publicity expert, who, with Rochelle Lefkowitz of Pro-Media, turned me into a best-selling author.

In particular, I want to thank the members of the Chicago chapter of the Association of Women Journalists and the *Chicago Tribune*, my long-term employer, for their support and encouragement.

PREFACE

The Career Coach is about the often harsh realities that we all face every day on the job—and how to handle them. I wrote this book so that when you encounter the hard times, you'll be able to find answers and advice that will help you solve career problems.

I like to think of this book as the Dr. Spock of employment, the book you grab when you're confused or stymied about what has happened and what to do next. Unlike Dr. Spock—and I hope he'll forgive me after all the help he gave me in raising three children—I lace many of my answers with humor. I wrote this book out of my own personal belief that it is better to laugh than to cry at the multitude of problems, snafus and roadblocks faced by working stiffs just like you and me eight hours a day, five days a week, 2,080 hours a year.

As you and I both know, there are many more rough times in our careers than smooth times. At least we seem to remember the rough ones and agonize over them much longer than the good things that happen! But I discuss much more than just the bad stuff we all know so well.

This book will not only help you find a job—and hopefully keep one—but will also help while

- going out on those dreaded job interviews;

- surviving while waiting for the results of your job interview;

- asking for a raise when salaries have been frozen;

- handling discrimination;

- balancing home and work responsibilities without collapsing;

- giving someone else a leg up; and

- surviving so-called structural changes—in other words, being fired.

I also give prescriptions for taking advantage of opportunities that open up for you—and how to get them to open. I talk about how to help others move along in their careers, a facet of work life that deeply appeals to me: We need each other.

The Career Coach is based on real-life job-hunting-and-keeping blues that I hear about every single day. The plaintive phone calls and letters that pour into my office keep me up-to-date on just how tough it is out there in the world of work. They make me so grateful for my job—which I love—that when I leave the office, I always ask someone to "save my place."

I know firsthand how scarce jobs are—at least the good ones—and how terrible it feels to be fired, especially when you hated the job anyway, and how difficult it is to be job hunting when you have no leverage because 60 other people are finalists for that one precious slot. I also know what becoming embroiled in office politics or the workplace jungle does to perfectly nice, apolitical people. And I know how little we as employees have to say about the factors that shape our daily lives, from access to prepaid gum surgery and root canals to access to better pay.

Comic relief is like extra-strength Tylenol® for employees in a tight job market, and I use it as often as I can in my columns, speeches and other public appearances. In the three decades that I have reported on employment issues, I have always found that if I combine the hard facts with humor, they are a little bit easier to swallow. That's why I usually begin my talks with this statement: "I'm very happy to be here. In fact, as someone who was the single working parent of three children, I'm happy to be anywhere!"

As the author of three nationally syndicated employment columns for the *Chicago Tribune*—"Women at work," "Jobs" and

"Your Job"—I know that when I intersperse humor with straight reporting about employment issues, I get an immediate and positive response. I hope this book will keep you going when all else, even the economy, fails. My hope is that it will save the sanity of people clearly ready to scream out loud in any crowded office, elevator or factory.

Read and enjoy!

PART ONE

How To Find a Top Job That's Right for You

1

What Is
the *Right* Job?

Welcome to the world of work! As your career coach, I will give you every bit of guidance and inside information you will need to help you win the right job and keep you in condition for a successful professional life. Together, we'll tone your job-searching muscles and get you in shape for the endurance test called Success. Together, I know we can do it.

Let the games begin!

You can't be a player in the job market of the 1990s and beyond without knowing what you want to do: Finding the right job is the warm-up for the rest of your career. With the constant restructuring of businesses and smart machines replacing workers wherever possible, no one will fault you for taking any job you can, especially if you and your family get hungry at least three times a day.

But the harsh facts of life in a job market riddled with downsizing—in other words, firings and layoffs—are that you're not going to last very long in a job that's wrong for you, especially if you hate it.

······················ *Coach's Tip* ·····················

One of the basic ingredients of the *right* job is enjoying what you do. It gives you a head start every day.
···

So for pragmatic reasons and your own personal happiness, it's worthwhile to find out what you really want to do within the framework of what jobs actually are available. That applies to you whether you're looking for your first job, seeking advancement in your present job or want to change careers.

It's extremely important to do what you like because, with the number of employees on staff cut to the bare bones—a trend that unfortunately will not go away—you'll get a chance to do so much of it!

······················ *Coach's Tip* ·····················

As part of your job-identification training program, take at least ten minutes each day for two weeks to think about what you really enjoy doing. Nothing is mystical or "touchy-feely" about the process, and it will help you determine if you've already made some pretty good decisions or if you want to make changes.
···

Some people say the best time to do this form of self-examination is on your way *to* work, while you're still fresh and before you become exhausted from doing all the things you don't like to do.

Here are some questions to ask yourself:

- Do you enjoy working with your hands?

- Do science and math challenge you?

- Does communications, entertainment or the media turn you on?

- Do you get excited when you think about the information superhighway?

- What about working with other people as opposed to working on your own?

- Do you prefer specific job assignments where you can see a beginning and an end—i.e., results you can point to?

- Does the idea of making Big Bucks make you happy?

- Do teaching, training or developing and helping others give you satisfaction?

- Do you enjoy organizing things, employing large doses of logic in your daily work?

- Do you prefer to proceed at a relaxed pace?

- Do you enjoy travel? Would you never complain about being on the road to get a job done?

- Are you a self-starter?

- Do you prefer being given a list or schedule of when to do what?

- Is it important to you to be involved in work you consider significant?

- Does it make you happy to help others, to be involved in close-to-the-heart social causes?

As you can see, none of these self-examination questions involves any learned skills. Instead, they are your baseline approach to the *right* job. You are what you do, and the best of all possible situations is to be able to do what you like, not just for your enjoyment but because you learn faster and simply do better if you don't dread going to work.

· · · · · · · · · · · · · · · ·   *Coach's Tip*   · · · · · · · · · · · · · · · ·

You may have other questions regarding your own personal likes. See where they, too, lead you.

· ·

Write down, or store in your personal computer, the things that make you *you*. If you feel you can't do the necessary groundwork on your own, which I believe you can, seek help from your high school, community college or college or university career counselor. Private, professional career counselors can be extremely helpful at this point, but be careful to check out their credentials and only pay on an hourly basis for services received. And don't pay up front. (See Chapter 2.)

Add to your list of what you like to do the things you really hate doing on the job. If you hate talking on the phone or answering letters, for example, those tasks probably are unavoidable in any profession, but at least you'll have them in front of you to remind you what to avoid, if possible. (Having a secretary, for instance, may solve both those problems.)

In a vacuum likes and dislikes about any job are empty. When you have honed in on what really counts in your life, turn to the back of the book and match your skills with my list of 100 best jobs for the 1990s and beyond. You'll probably see several good "fits," and then it will be up to you to pursue your choices.

· · · · · · · · · · · · · · · · · *Coach's Tip* · · · · · · · · · · · · · · · ·

Don't be afraid to explore several jobs; it's a way of hedging your bets in a tight and constantly changing job market. And the fact remains that in all likelihood you will change professions three times and jobs at least six times over your work life.

· ·

The important thing is to try to make sure that each time a change appears on the horizon *you* are the one choosing the profession or the job and it *is* the right one for you, at least for the time being.

During a radio show I recently was on, a caller said he was in computer technology and had entered the field six years ago because he wanted to be in a secure profession. But during that time, as computer technology changed, his specialty became obsolete. He had changed jobs four times, working with different employers until each had computer systems—smart machines—that were programmed to do the work for which he had been responsible.

He said, "I'm tired of changing jobs. I know that technology, in particular computer programming, is the best field for me, in addition to being a growing one. And it pays fairly well. But how do I find the *right* job?"

I told him—gently—that looking for that one right job for a lifetime career isn't enough in today's labor market and that there is no such thing as job security. What he should look for is *one* right job at a time, just as he had been doing without being aware of it. I congratulated him for being skilled and experienced in computer science because it is, as he knows, a job with a future.

I then urged the caller to take charge of his career. I encouraged him to keep up with the technological changes in his field, to learn as many computer programs as possible and to become an expert systems analyst. I coached him by saying I understood his search for something to hold on to professionally. But I added that it probably wouldn't come from working for one employer. He might do better to think of becoming an independent consultant, advising a variety of firms on their current computer needs. And then, when businesses outgrow the need for that advice, to look for a new aspect of computer technology to consult about, one that the speeding information superhighway surely will supply.

In other words, since job security is no longer a given, why not do something you really like doing while you're doing it?

· · · · · · · · · · · · · · · · *Coach's Tip* · · · · · · · · · · · · · · · ·

In addition to requisite skills and particular job characteristics, another component of the right job is job satisfaction. You deserve it.

· ·

What makes you happy at work? In the list of questions earlier in this chapter that I suggest you ask yourself regarding desirable job characteristics, only one question pertains to satisfaction, the one that asks if you like to make Big Bucks. I assume you do, but there are other factors, too, if present, that can change your workday from a nightmare to a satisfying way to spend your time.

Ask yourself the following questions to ascertain what gives you a sense of gratification and accomplishment:

- How important are praise and recognition to you in doing your job?

- How often do you think you should be promoted?

- How much job security do you need to function? Do you need to know in advance that your job will be there for the next five years (you can't expect much longer than that) in order to be able to perform well?

- Does the attractiveness of the physical plant or office where you work matter? Do you feel your productivity is affected by the quality of the workplace?

- Are you looking for friends in the workplace or simply 9 to 5 colleagues? If the people you work with are not congenial or helpful, will that be a constant, daily thorn in your side?

- In addition to a good salary (the Big Bucks mentioned earlier), how important are benefits and perks? If you're considering part-time work, this question is particularly important.

You now have a handle on some of the ingredients that make up the right job for you. For the most part, these ingredients are based on your own personal hopes and desires. The next thing to look at is what personality traits will be required of you—in addition to your skills and learning—to succeed in your chosen work.

·················· *Coach's Tip* ··················

The most important quality is flexibility. The *American Heritage Dictionary* defines *flexible* as "pliable, capable of or responsive to change, adaptable."

··

That, of course, is accurate, but another definition listed as its core meaning is more to the point: "capable of withstanding stress without injury." It's pertinent because if you can't handle the stress of change, the "injury" will be that you will not find the *right* job.

Flexibility also means being able to roll with the changes, to accept constant alterations in the way you do your work and to be ready to go on to the next job when your current one disappears. Flexibility also includes eagerness—not resistance—to learning new ways to work. It means a career-long commitment to learning and growing. (See Chapter 14.) It means your education does not end with formal training.

That's asking a lot of people, but if you are prepared to cope with the radical employment changes precipitated by the technological revolution, you'll be a much happier worker and far more likely to find the *right* job.

To mitigate the disappointment of finally getting a job in your profession only to find out you really hate every minute of it, it's important to learn as much as possible about the job's characteristics *before* you begin your actual job search.

················ *Coach's Tip* ················

One good training technique to avoid the hazard of entering the wrong field is to do informational interviews with professionals already in the field.

··

When I say "informational interviews," that's exactly what I mean. Too many people use that title as a mask for asking for a job. That's all right to do, but it's not *informational interviewing,* in which you briefly meet with a professional or talk over the phone to find out what you can about the field in general. It's a form of networking that is extremely helpful in the early stages of job hunting.

One of the rules of informational interviewing is never, but never, ask the person talking to you for a job. That's unforgivable and not fair play. And it won't work. The people who usually are kind enough to take time to clue you in about the realities of the profession rarely do the hiring. Another way to find out in advance whether or not you're headed in the right direction is to work summers, vacations or weekends, if possible, at any level in the field of your choice. This gives you a powerful leg up on finding the right job.

Another good career exercise is serving an internship, paid or unpaid. It also counts as experience on your resume. Potential employers eye internships with approval because they send the message that you care enough to sacrifice your leisure time for your career.

If you're still in school, seriously consider cooperative education, which also counts on your resume. If you enroll in a post-secondary-education cooperative program, your classroom work will be coordinated by your school with an actual job with a local employer that is related to whatever you're studying.

Cooperative education students are among the first to know that they either love or hate their chosen field. For more information about cooperative education, contact the Cooperative Education Association, 3311 Toledo Terrace, Hyattsville, MD 20782; 301-559-8850.

················· *Coach's Tip* ················

Another way to get inside information before actually moving inside the workplace is to do some sort of volunteer work. (Also see Chapter 16.)

···

Volunteer work in a field that fascinates you, from offering to do a newsletter for a for-profit accounting firm to feeding the animals at a nonprofit zoo, gives you an up-close picture of what it's really like to work in a particular profession.

If you're interested in health care, for instance, consider volunteering at a hospital, nursing home, public health clinic or any other health-care facility that accepts volunteers. Health care is a burnout profession, and after volunteering, you may opt to get out before you get in. On the other hand, you may see that a job in health care is the right one for you.

···············   *Coach's Tip*   ················

A secret to positioning yourself for the right job is to find out everything in advance that you can about the day-to-day work involved and conditions in the actual worksite.

··

I've been coaching you in what to do in the best of all possible worlds, where there indeed are jobs that match your basic requirements and employers who are eager to hire you. That world does exist for many well-trained, highly skilled people, and we're all very happy for them. Though it absolutely is necessary to figure out what makes you the most happy worker in the world, it's only part of the work you have to do to find the right job for you.

The rest comes when you realistically see that you might not be able to start out in the absolutely right job; or perhaps it doesn't exist. That's when you have to rev up your motors and use your considerable energy to find the right job that will lead you to the right job.

Hopefully, employers will be standing in long lines at your doorstep, begging you to come to work for them and do whatever makes you the most happy. Even more hopefully, they will pay whatever you ask and promote you rapidly. I'd like that to be the way your job search turns out. But just in case it doesn't—and most likely, it won't—you have to be prepared.

In other words, what I'm talking about is that *now* is the time to start facing the fact that you have to get real.

Aiming for the heights will prepare you well for finding any route whatsoever to get there. Knowing what you want, what satisfies you and makes you happy, is a strong base from which to start because it equips you with a shield of endurance and determination that eventually will pay off for you in a big way.

···············   *Coach's Tip*   ················

Don't discard all the knowledge you've gained from learning about yourself and the right job for you. Use it as the bottom line to get your career started. It will stand you in good stead because you will have a goal in sight.

··

I'm sure you've read the many stories about the McDonald's executives who started out working at the fast-food counter and about the honchos at Walgreens who began their careers running errands. These stories are true, and there are thousands of them. Even Gilbert and Sullivan in the operetta *H.M.S. Pinafore* literally sang the praises of the admiral who started out by "polishing the handle of the big front door." He polished up the handle so carefully that "now he is ruler of the Queen's Navee!"

Today such efforts no longer are called "starting at the bottom." Instead they're called "grunt work." Whatever the name, it's a good starting point for job seekers, job changers and career seekers.

The main reason that the bottom is a good place to start is that entry-level jobs are available in every field—but middle-management, executive jobs no longer are. While some training and management jobs are available, there simply aren't enough to go around. That's why you probably won't start at the top or even in the middle, despite work experience or training. (See Chapter 11.) Today you probably will have to start at the bottom and work your way up.

················· *Coach's Tip* ·················

Don't take it personally if you're offered a job you feel is beneath your capabilities. You may want to consider taking it, especially if nothing else is out there in your field and the job is with a company you've thoroughly researched and know you'd like to work for.

···

"Sitting at a clerical desk buying time or space doing grunt work while waiting for an opening inside that company is better than being on the outside," said Victor R. Lindquist, former associate dean and director of placement at Northwestern University. The recently retired Lindquist conducted an annual survey of 264 U.S. businesses to ascertain how many college graduates they planned to hire and what they would pay them. So when the veteran employment expert advises lowering your sights if necessary—but only temporarily—it's a good idea to listen.

"Some people, even students·with a brand-new degree, may start in the mailroom," the former placement director said. "After all, it's better to be sitting on the bench in the ballpark than looking in through a hole in the fence." Lindquist reminds us that starting at the bottom and working your way up are "very much a part of the work culture. But in the last several decades, the expectation was for college graduates, at least, that they would go into training programs and move up from one spot to another to get ready for an important job."

But not anymore, he says. "Today you have to go in and take what they have. Say it's advertising. You know that's where you want to be, but the agencies you want to work for aren't recruiting and there's no training program this year. But wait a minute—they do have a job. It offers only hourly wages, and it's buying space for clients."

Lindquist's advice: "Take it. You're inside. If you know where you want to go and the road leads in that direction, start walking and then begin running." He sums up the situation this way: "If you want to work for the devil, you have to spend some time in hell. It's called paying your dues."

Lindquist may be teasing you a bit, but he makes a good point that you have to start somewhere. And spending some time in "hell" won't be forever.

·················· *Coach's Tip* ··················

Remember that the right job for you is one you can get.
···

2

Preparing To Find a Job—Kicking Your Resume Dependency

The first thing people think of when they decide to start job hunting is that they must put together a resume or update their old one. That's a good thought—and it's the right thought. But the one that comes next is the one that worries me. Most job seekers think that if they have a good resume and send it to enough people, they'll get a job without ever having to do anything else.

Unfortunately, that's not the way it works, especially in a fiercely competitive labor market where employers get so many resumes that they often dump most of them without ever reading them. If you enjoy sending out hundreds of resumes a week and spending a lot of money on postage—whether or not you get any replies—then go ahead and do so. It certainly will keep you busy! But it is much wiser and faster to kick your resume dependency habit and use the resume in the way that it can work best for you.

· · · · · · · · · · · · · · · · ·   *Coach's Tip*   · · · · · · · · · · · · · · · · ·

A resume may get you a job lead—though that is rare—
or a job interview, which is its actual purpose. But it cannot
get you a job. Not by itself.

· ·

A resume is indeed the place to start when you know what
you want to do and where you want to work. (See Chapter 3.)
Creating a resume—but not one that's too "creative"—is an excellent starting point. By putting your resume together, you not
only have a valuable tool for your job hunt, but you also have
another opportunity to analyze your strengths and weaknesses
and your hopes for the future.

To make your resume work for you, you need to put together
a general resume that includes your work experience, education
and special skills. That will be your prototype resume, and when
you do your homework (see Chapter 3), you will be able to key
it to each particular company and the individual in that company whose attention you're trying to get.

Your general, "baseline" resume is a job-hunting treasure that
you will use and reuse over the life of your successful career. But
it's not a crutch. It's important to put in the necessary time and
effort to make it the best, most reliable source of your professional life.

· · · · · · · · · · · · · · · · ·   *Coach's Tip*   · · · · · · · · · · · · · · · · ·

A resume is your own personal identification card. It is
not a passport.

· ·

While you're organizing the information for your resume,
keep in mind that the actual resume itself will be only one page.
Employers, human resource executives and other interviewers
don't have time to look at anything longer than that. Human
resource departments also have had cutbacks in staff, and no
one has time to read two pages or more. Additionally, there is

such a severe job crisis—one which will continue into the 21st century—that employers are swamped with resumes.

•••••••••••••••• *Coach's Tip* ••••••••••••••••••

Y̲ou have a better chance of having your resume read if it's only one page. You can add all the other details you don't have room for in person—when you have the face-to-face interview a top-notch, one-page resume will get you.
••

That one-page resume also should be printed on plain white paper, not red, blue or shocking pink. It's true that those colors will get you attention, but not the kind you want. Human resource personnel are not interested in anything different or fancy. They just want the facts. They don't have time for anything but serious business when they're trying to fill a job. A listing of where you worked and when, in chronological order, followed by your educational background, is the only resume I recommend.

For many years, when employees were scarce and jobs plentiful, two other types of resumes emerged: the functional resume and the historical resume.

The *functional resume* is a list of your actual skills and experiences, without any dates or names of previous employers. It is an excellent format for someone who has been out of the job market for a long time and doesn't want a potential employer to know that immediately.

The *historical,* or *anecdotal resume,* is best described as an informal letter, telling the employer who you are, what you can do, your strengths and interests. This works well for people who have changed jobs often and are concerned that employers will rule them out because of their work history. Before firing became a way of life in corporate America, some people who had been discharged used the historical resume to cover up that fact. For people who are good communicators, who can sell themselves verbally, the informal resume allows them to present themselves in their best light.

I like both the functional and historical resumes because they give a little leverage to the job seeker who otherwise would have very little chance to be taken seriously. But what you and I may like doesn't matter. It's the employer who must be served. And employers tell me they no longer have the time to wallow through creative verbiage. They want the facts without any frills.

Though there is much reporting of the use of video resumes, employers tell me they don't have time for them, either. And I, for one, do not like them, but if you want to give them a try, I would say go ahead and make a video of yourself describing your work experience. But once again, keep it short. And don't invest too much money in it.

I also want to caution you about the high-tech networks that send your resumes out online throughout the world. They're an excellent idea but are not focused in the way you need to be to make your resume work for you. But, if you have the money, sign up and use them for extra exposure. But never let them be your only source of potential jobs.

There's something else employers also demand from job applicants: the truth. Don't lie on your resume for any reason whatsoever. Because employers are concerned about hiring anyone who may turn out to be a legal liability, they're spending the time and money to check resumes.

Employers have plenty of time to check out everything on your resume because they are in no hurry to fill an opening. The longer they delay, the more money they save—another fact of life in a work world where executives get credit for paring their staffs to the bone.

When employers check to find out if you've ever stolen a car, robbed a bank or welshed on your debts—all serious matters — they also may turn up the fact that you never graduated from the college you listed, enrolled in advanced courses, ran an entire department, flew a hot-air balloon or other such fudgings.

Whether the lie is an all-time pernicious one or a mild distortion of the truth, the end result is the same: You will not get the job. So if you have no moral compunctions about lying on your resume, be pragmatic and don't do it. You will be caught, sooner or later.

In an era where teamwork and flexibility are stressed by employers, your lack of what you think are the proper credentials may not matter as much as you think it does. Character counts, too. And that will come out in the job interview. (See Chapter 4.)

································ *Coach's Tip* ·················

Tell the truth and nothing but the truth.

··

Because you will have to change your resume for every interview you line up (see Chapter 4), create it on a computer so that you'll be able to modify it without starting from scratch. You'll also be able to print out as many copies as you need.

The most important thing about the resume is what it tells a personnel officer about you. The second most important thing is that now you have in front of you, in concise form, your actual work history and experience. Though not as historic, perhaps, as the Declaration of Independence, the resume is a very serious piece of paper.

But it's not the only piece of paper that you must prepare with diligence. The cover letter is equally important. Many employment experts say the cover letter may be even more important because it is what job interviewers see first and may or may not influence them to keep reading.

I've asked human resource people which is more important, the cover letter or the resume. Most answer that the resume is what counts. They say they always will at least glance at the resume even if the cover letter is unimpressive or off-target. But an impressive cover letter, they agree, will help your chances of getting an interview when your resume shows that your skills are pretty much like everyone else's.

················ *Coach's Tip* ·················

A good cover letter will help you stand out from the crowd of applicants. So make sure your cover letter is good.

··

Just as the content of a good resume has changed over the years, so has the information you should put in your cover letter. This also should be brief—not more than a paragraph—as hard as that may sound to do.

In the 1980s you could have written a cover letter like the following and probably have gotten a response:

Dear Employment Interviewer:

All my life I've dreamed of working for a company that has the excellent reputation that yours does. I have watched your growth with awe over the years, and there's nothing I want more than to be part of your organization.

I'm willing to start anywhere, just to be able to get my foot in the door of your outstanding firm. I am a quick learner, loyal and honest. You will never be sorry that you hired me.

Sincerely yours,
A Really Naive Job Seeker

Today that kind of cover letter goes right in the trash, along with your unread resume. Times have changed, and most employers are not interested in your hopes or dreams. They don't even care whether or not you have a high regard for the company—at least not in the cover letter.

They already know you want to work for them. That's why you are applying for a job, right? So skip the accolades and save them for the job interview.

Being willing to start anywhere is unacceptable. You must know what job you are applying for. You also must know what department you want to work in. And most importantly, you must be able to spell out up front, in the cover letter, what you can do for the company that will affect its bottom line in a positive way.

Nobody cares that you are a quick learner. They don't intend to teach you the basic skills of the job. You must come prepared to do the job from the first day. And even mentioning that you are loyal and honest is so archaic these days that it might even raise suspicions about your loyalty and honesty and why you even mentioned them.

·················· *Coach's Tip* ················

Don't ask what the company can do for you. Explain, in one paragraph, what you can do for it.

···

Here's a sample cover letter that has a good chance of getting a response:

Dear Employment Interviewer:

I am applying for your advertised job of mall manager. I have been involved with city and suburban malls for 10 years and know that I can increase your merchant base to 75 stores from 50 stores and your annual earnings to $1.25 billion from $1 billion.

I'm looking forward to discussing my ideas with you in person.

Sincerely yours,
A Really Savvy Job Seeker

Use the cover letter to establish yourself as a serious job seeker who already understands the needs and goals of the company and, when hired, can hit the ground running. And convey this information once again on a piece of white stationery, preferably one with your letterhead on it.

If you feel that such a brief resume and even briefer cover letter do not adequately describe your attributes, note at the bottom of your resume that another page is appended that includes special things about you that you want the interviewer to know. You might want to include on this extra page such things as the fact that you put yourself through college, have served in the U.S. armed forces (some employers may qualify for a special tax deduction for hiring veterans), are active in a community group (so long as it's not political, it's okay to mention it) or have a particularly fascinating hobby.

The extra page may or may not get read. When you do get an interview set up, it would be wise to act as if no one knows any of these extra facets of your life, so be sure to bring them up face-to-face.

There are some things you absolutely never should include in your resume, cover letter or any extra information because they have nothing to do with your qualifications for the job and employers are forbidden by law to ask questions about them in advance of offering you a job. They include such details as your age, race, ethnic background, religion, sexual orientation, marital status or health, including disabilities. Various groups have fought for decades to eliminate these questions from job interviews and finally have succeeded. So don't play into the possible prejudices of your future employers by giving out this information in advance.

·············· *Coach's Tip* ················

Never include a photo with your resume.
···

One of the reasons I'm not overly enthusiastic about the video resume is that employers may see at a glance that they don't want to hire you, and can easily get away with discriminating against you.

Here are some more no-nos:

- Don't include references; simply note that you will supply them.

- Never mention salaries you have earned in the past or hope to earn in the future. If you answer an ad that requests your salary history, reply that you will furnish it in person.

- Don't help the interviewer rule you out before ever meeting you.

When you're satisfied with your resume and the cover letter, the next step is to send them out. I'll explain the details of how to do that in the next chapter, but for now I want to encourage you to remain somewhat conservative in your method of delivering the goods.

••••••••••••••••• *Coach's Tip* •••••••••••••••••

Don't even think of doing anything flamboyant to get your resume to a potential employer. In other words, no tricks.

•••

I've heard countless stories of job seekers who have sent their resumes with helium balloons delivered by 1,000 clowns. I've heard the stories about sending resumes with boxes of candy and huge bouquets of flowers. I've even heard of one job candidate who sent his resume in the mouth of his well-trained golden retriever.

I've heard stories of people parachuting onto the building that contains their potential employers and delivering their resume in a grand manner. Over the years I've also heard of job applicants stepping out of cakes, resumes in hand, and of sending a three-piece band to serenade the personnel officer interviewing them.

I've heard all these stories, and I love every one of them. The only problem is I've never heard that the person behind those tricks got the job. And getting the job is the point of all the work you've done preparing to get the job.

••••••••••••••••• *Coach's Tip* •••••••••••••••••

While the resume is the most important tool in your equipment bag, it's not the whole game. There are other things you must begin doing in order to get the right job.

•••

If you haven't already done so, now is the time to join networks and professional associations. (Note the plural.) The more organizations you join, the more contacts you will make and the more access you will have to information about job openings. Join groups that are devoted entirely to your area of professional interest and skills. Join groups that have a variety of members from a variety of fields.

Join business clubs and discussion groups. Sign up for community groups and other volunteer activities that interest you. You can't fake interest in volunteer work because your involvement is so personal.

At each of these groups, network. Offer to help other people track down information about their work; doing so allows *you* to ask for help. And don't be too shy to ask for tips and leads. If you don't ask, you won't receive. Be active in these groups. Volunteer for everything.

And you don't need a group to network. Talk to your friends, acquaintances, REALTOR®, landlord, insurance representative, accountant, financial planner, hair stylist, supermarket checker, bus driver, elevator operator, car mechanic, plumber, carpenter, painter, electrician and every salesperson who ever waits on you.

Once you've established yourself as a colleague, friend or helpful stranger, you will be able to ask all these people direct, incisive questions about how they can help you when you decide to go after a particular job.

············· *Coach's Tip* ················

If you can't find a network that fills your professional needs, form one yourself. Name yourself president—and put it on your resume.

··

You're all set and ready to start on your job hunt, but first you may want to set up an in-person meeting with a career counselor. Expert guidance at this point may give you the jump start your job search needs, but you must be extremely careful about whom you see.

You can get good advice—at no cost or very low fees—through your local high school or community college. If you're currently enrolled at an institution of higher learning, make an appointment with a counselor in its career placement center. If you're a graduate, you can still go back to your school and get help—without charge.

Outside of educational institutions, private consultants are difficult to evaluate. Some are involved in scams where they charge you thousands of dollars in advance and promise you "access to the hidden job market."

················· *Coach's Tip* ·················

Run like crazy when you're promised "access to the hidden job market." You may find that all you get is a list of companies to send resumes to—a list you could have found in any library.

··

Don't sign a contract to pay a lump sum of money in advance to a career counselor. Pay only for services that you want, on a piecemeal basis; if you're not allowed to do that, take your business elsewhere. Career counselors give advice; they don't find you jobs. Avoid those who promise to do so.

Qualified career counselors charge on an hourly basis. Many of them have degrees in counseling and psychology. Their fees range from $45 to $75 an hour. If they are certified by the National Board for Certified Counselors, 3 D Terrace Way, Greensboro, NC 27403; 910-547-0607, you know they are both skilled and ethical.

It's also wise to check out the credentials and reputation of career counselors with your local Better Business Bureau.

However, the best source I know is Stuart Alan Rado, a nationally known consumer advocate who acts as the watchdog of career marketers. Send a self-addressed, stamped envelope to Rado, 1500 W. 23d Street, Sunset Island, #3, Miami Beach, FL 33140; 305-532-2607, and he will alert you to the people to keep away from.

Now, to keep in shape for your job hunt, the next step is to do your homework.

················· *Coach's Tip* ·················

Treat yourself to something wonderful, and don't think about your job hunt—for 24 hours.

··

3

Doing Your Homework—What Really Pays Off

Deciding on the field of your choice, and the job you want in that field, and then preparing your resume and laying some of the groundwork for a successful job search were demanding tasks, but what you have just completed are only conditioning exercises. Now come the warm-ups. And that means doing your homework.

Doing your homework means getting all the information you can in advance about what job opportunities exist. It means being so smart, so well informed about the companies that are hiring that when you actually do send out your resume, it's right on target and you're not spinning your wheels helplessly. Nothing should be haphazard about hunting for a job in today's employment market. Doing your homework means minimizing your disappointments right now and maximizing your chances of getting the right job right now.

You should feel extremely confident and in good shape, because you know you've done everything correctly up to this point. Hopefully, that momentum will propel you into the hard work of completing the next step of your job hunt.

Doing your homework means hard work—a lot of it—but it's all part of the game of Success.

·················· *Coach's Tip* ·················

Start by reading the classified ads in the newspaper. I'm not urging you to do so because I happen to work for a major daily newspaper—though that's not such a bad reason—but because that's where the majority of jobs, at every level, in every field, are listed.

··

In the classified sections of newspapers, both local and national, and of magazines, you'll find job openings you'll want to pursue. By reading them you'll not only get good leads but also a broader picture of the current labor market. You'll see what fields are hot, who is advertising and for what kind of jobs. From the tone of the ads, the way they're worded, you'll be able to get a feel for how certain industries and individual employers regard job candidates.

·················· *Coach's Tip* ·················

If the ad seems too cold to you or too distant or too superior, forget it—even if it's in your field. Your gut instincts are telling you it's not the place for you to consider working.

··

Keep a folder of jobs you know at a glance are ones you want to pursue. Mark the folder "A-1" or "Best Bets" or "Great Expectations." Also keep a secondary file of jobs that you already know have some negatives for you but might be worth pursuing if you run out of first choices. Mark this file "Maybe" or "Later" or "Here's Hoping." But don't discard them: they may come in handy sooner than you think.

Classified ads don't have a long shelf life. Begin reading and collecting them the day you decide to look for your first job, change jobs or switch careers. But be aware that if you don't go after them immediately, they may not be there when you decide to start your full-court press for a job.

················· *Coach's Tip* ·················

Even if an ad is old, keep the name of the company on file if the job was particularly appealing. You will want to research that company further when you start your actual job search in case there are other opportunities somewhere within the firm. And since companies are so slow to hire these days, there's an outside chance that the job opening may be viable even months later or that the person hired didn't work out.

···

Classified ads are an essential source for your job search, but they're not the only ones. After you've carefully studied them and have a feel for the job market in general and for your segment of it in particular, start aggressively exploring your other options.

················· *Coach's Tip* ·················

Network, network, network! With everyone, everywhere. Ask if they know of any job openings in your field. Ask for names and phone numbers of people to call about a job. Don't be obnoxious and don't sound desperate, but get the word out. Don't be shy.

···

Your family and friends are your first targets in networking. Next come colleagues, friends of friends and people with whom you personally do business. Now is the time to stand up at meetings of associations or other formal networks and state exactly what you're looking for. At your volunteer groups and community meetings, touch base with acquaintances—especially those on the board of directors—and ask for job leads.

·················· *Coach's Tip* ··················

If people don't know of specific job openings, ask them for names of contacts inside the industry or particular companies you're interested in.
··

Job banks often have good leads. If any group you belong to has one, read the listings thoroughly. The leads you get will be focused in your particular field, and the potential employers probably will be much more receptive to you simply because you're part of the association. While I personally don't recommend you place a job-wanted ad in a general newspaper or magazine, it's a good idea to do so in newsletters or magazines of professional associations or networks. Employers tell me they carefully read those ads but rarely the ads in newspapers.

·················· *Coach's Tip* ··················

If you place an advertisement for yourself, keep it straight and to the point. Once again, no tricks.
··

Two more sources for jobs are your local state employment office and your local community college. You pay for both with your taxes, so don't be reluctant to ask for help. If you're unemployed and receiving workers' compensation, the state has already made you aware of its resources.

·················· *Coach's Tip* ··················

State job banks contain thousands of job openings for anyone seeking a job. Additionally, state employment offices have national job listings, and it's important to examine them as well. And while you're there, get some job tips from a state employment counselor, whose services also are available to everyone.
··

Community colleges offer both career guidance and local job listings. Touching base with them is helpful because in the process you may learn you are just one skill or one course short of being qualified for the job of your dreams.

If you're a college graduate—no matter how long ago you were graduated—contact the head of the department your degree is in and ask for a list of job leads. Smart employers often ask department heads for names of possible job candidates. Since many academicians also work as private consultants, they have excellent contacts and also are on the cutting edge of what's happening in your field.

For even broader job opportunities to explore, go to your college placement centers. Even if you've never paid your alumni dues, they will have to help you. And they can. Most college centers have up-to-date job banks plus a wealth of information about every aspect of job hunting. After all, when you land a good job, it makes them look good! Even if you're taking only one course at the institution or never completed your degree, you still have access to this veritable fountainhead of information.

················· *Coach's Tip* ·················

If you're currently enrolled in any educational institution at any level, make its guidance center your second home and the counselors who run it your best friends. Their assignment is to help you find a job.

··

In your quest for jobs, jobs, jobs—a full-time job in itself— don't fall victim to a job scam. One way to avoid this trap is never, ever pay for a job. In the previous chapter I warned you about unscrupulous career marketers and how to identify them.

Another kind of scam, an unfortunate offshoot of the global marketplace in which you will be working, involves working abroad. A job overseas is an exciting idea, but don't be fooled by ads that ask for money up front and promise you a job. Too often, once your money is in hand the "employment agency" disappears, never to be found again anywhere in the world.

Working overseas, especially if you're proficient in another language or want to become so, is a smart career move, but bona fide jobs are scarce unless you work for a corporation and it sends you on one of its prized foreign assignments. Other than having such an inside track, the best way to get the chance to live in a new and stimulating environment while having your employer pay you to do so is to get a job overseas through the *International Employment Hotline.*

What I like about the *Hotline,* which is a monthly newsletter filled with job opportunities throughout the world, is that the publication carries no ads. Each job listed is thoroughly checked out by Will Cantrell, its publisher. In his consumer's guide to jobs overseas, Cantrell accepts no ads from employers. He lists only the jobs he personally knows are for real.

Among the jobs recently listed were working with refugees in Thailand, teaching English as a second language in Indonesia, working for the United Nations in Rome and teaching vocational skills to petrochemical workers in Saudi Arabia. Every time I recommend Cantrell's newsletter, I get oceans of thanks from readers. To subscribe to the newsletter, which costs $36 annually, write to *International Employment Hotline,* P.O. Box 3030, Oakton, VA 22124.

Meanwhile, back on the mainland, you still have to go after every possible avenue of job opportunity. Many job seekers are registering with computerized on-line networks of job listings or, more informally, using on-line networks to ask everyone out there in cyberspace if they know about a good job opening. According to *The Wall Street Journal,* the Self-Placement Network, Inc. in New York, not only sends resumes out to seven major on-line networks used by 16 million people in 145 countries, but it also searches weekly for job leads among 110,000 listings in electronic job banks and classified ads put on-line by 55 major newspapers.

Also find out if your college, vocational institution or professional association is part of an on-line job bank and—before you sign up—what it costs to join.

On-line job searches give you a great deal of extra exposure, but don't count on them alone to get you a job—no matter how much of a computer devotee you are. One problem is that the responses most likely will be so broad based and general that you will have to spend hours of additional research to ascertain if there actually is anything in it for you to pursue. However, a job lead is a job lead, and your trusty computer may lead you to a job without your ever leaving home.

If you're currently doing temporary work—a good idea for short-term income and a chance to look around at the business world up front and close—ask about job openings. You're inside already, and it isn't unprofessional to ask the person in the human resources department who brought you aboard if any full-time positions in your area of interest are open.

If you're serving an internship, have a part-time job or are involved in a cooperative education program, you've probably already shown how capable you are. So don't hesitate to ask your supervisor and your colleagues if they know of any job openings or if anyone has plans to leave. Also ask if they have heard of any opportunities elsewhere in the industry or can give you names of people to contact.

· · · · · · · · · · · · · · · · · *Coach's Tip* · · · · · · · · · · · · · · · ·

Being on the inside, even if it's only on a temporary or part-time basis, is one of the greatest advantages a job seeker who is not currently employed can have.

· ·

Now and then you'll see job fairs advertised in the papers. If the jobs mentioned are what you've been looking for, go. Many people get job interviews from attending job fairs. But even when no specific job catches your eye, if an employer you want to talk to about your specialty is going to have a booth at the fair, go anyway. It's a good way to get names of people to talk to.

Job clubs also are extremely effective. Many churches, community groups, libraries and even your state employment office sponsor them. Job clubs are an intensive form of networking. Composed of 15 to 20 people looking for jobs, they offer support, job leads and motivation. They're generally free or charge only a small fee. Each member stays in the group until the last person gets a job, and knowing that is the setup gives many job seekers the sense of security they need.

················· *Coach's Tip* ················

It's important for many job seekers to know they are not alone, and job clubs help them get through the daily stress of looking for a job. And the best part is that they do help you find a job.

···

Last on my list of how to access the job market are employment agencies, which you would expect to be first. My concern about employment agencies is that they usually don't get paid until they fill the job. (*Warning:* Never use an employment agency that asks you to pay part or all of a fee; the employer should pay.) That means they can't possibly be looking out for your best interests, only the employer's. I get scores of phone calls from people who have been sent out on job interviews by employment agencies for work they can't or don't ever want to do—and for a salary that is well below what they rightfully expect to make.

If an employment agency advertises a job you want and it actually has that job opening when you get there, go after it. But don't expect the agency to make the right fit. You'll have to do that yourself.

Executive recruiters also are people who do not work for you; they represent only the corporations and businesses that hire them to fill job openings. They also are called *headhunters.*

Almost every day I get calls or letters from job seekers who want to know the name of a good executive recruiter who can get them a job. I explain that headhunters don't work that way. They only seek to fill the openings their clients have; they don't work to get you, the job seeker, a job. Headhunters deal only with executive openings, too, because that's where the money is.

Nevertheless it's a good idea to send your resume to executive recruiters in your field because they know the market extremely well. Most will file your resume, and if anything comes up that you might be qualified for, they'll call you. The most efficient way to utilize executive search firms is to send your resume to headhunters who specialize in your line of work. The best source for that information is John Sibbald's book, *The New Career Makers* (Harper Business, $28). Sibbald, who heads his own executive search firm, has compiled the book to analyze those who are tops in the profession, and he groups them by specialty. Those groupings are invaluable to job seekers.

·················· *Coach's Tip* ················

If a headhunter calls and wants to meet with you, say yes, even if you currently are employed, have a job lined up, are not looking for another job or think you are too busy to talk to an executive recruiter.

··

You may get a job lead out of the meeting; but even if you don't, you can use the occasion to find out what's happening in your profession, where the jobs are, what the salaries are, what the future looks like and whatever else you want to know. In return, even if you're not interested in pursuing a particular opening the headhunter is trying to fill, if you suggest names of other colleagues or acquaintances for the headhunter to contact, you will have earned your lunch and the headhunter's gratitude.

················ *Coach's Tip* ·············

Always be polite and helpful to executive recruiters. They never forget either a rudeness or a favor.

···

As much misunderstanding as there is about headhunters, there's even more about outplacement agencies. Part of the confusion comes from the nomenclature. *Outplacement* suggests to many job seekers that the service being offered is job placement, but they do not find you a job.

For the most part, *outplacement consultants* are hired by the same people who hire executive recruiters: employers. Their assignment is to help fired employees design a job search and to provide counseling, office space and secretarial staff. (See Chapter 12.) A few outplacement services will help you on an individual basis, and their services are worthwhile—if you can afford the fees.

Now that you have used every possible source of information about job openings, it's time to do some research about the field that interests you, potential employers, possible openings, salaries and geographical locations. This is called *doing your homework.*

By hitting the business books and professional magazines at your local or school library and by sitting in front of a computer and calling up the databases that give you the information you need, you will find a wealth of information that will give your job search a clear focus.

In addition to finding out the name of the chief executive, if the company does indeed hire people in your field, learn all you can about the firm's financial outlook (extremely important these days) and information about their goods and services. This way you will be able efficiently to target sending your resumes to the right companies, rather than using a scattershot approach that rarely works.

················· *Coach's Tip* ·················

Look at the doing-your-homework phase of your job search as the marketing of You.

···

While hitting the books—and the computers, too—find out what's happening in your profession. Who are the heavy hitters? Select some companies you're interested in that are located in your geographical area of choice, though you will have to be flexible about the city or state in which you work. Study their financial outlook, personnel policies and whatever other inside information you can garner.

And don't just research Fortune 500 companies. Businesses with 50 or fewer employees are doing most of the hiring today.

················· *Coach's Tip* ·················

If quality of life is high on your must-have list, check out the company's work and family benefits.

···

With the passage in 1993 of the Family and Medical Leave Act (FMLA), the federal government mandates 12 weeks of unpaid leave each year for employees in firms with 50 or more workers. If you have worked for the same employer for at least 1,250 hours for one year preceding the leave, the FMLA guarantees your current or an equivalent position when you return from caring for a newborn, adopted child, sick family member or your own serious health condition that prevents you from doing your job. But forward-looking companies also offer their employees other benefits. More and more firms have elder-care and child-care referral services; others offer child-care reimbursement or actually sponsor day-care centers. Forward-looking companies give options that make a difference in getting through the day, such as job sharing and flexible hours. Many offer cafeteria benefits, so you can choose among the insurance protections, tax deductions and investment savings options (such as salary reduction plans, profit-sharing plans, etc.) that best serve your needs.

· · · · · · · · · · · · · · · · · *Coach's Tip* · · · · · · · · · · · · · · · · ·

Do your homework first. If these matters are extremely important to you, find out about them *before* applying for a job, *not* by asking potential employers—at least not in the early stages of the job interview.

· ·

From your research you'll be able to compile a list of companies that not only interest you but actually may be hiring. It is the time to start sending out your resumes, targeted to a particular company, a particular person in the company and a particular job. Rewrite your resume for each job you want to pursue.

· · · · · · · · · · · · · · · · · *Coach's Tip* · · · · · · · · · · · · · · · · ·

Now your resume is working for you. Take your time while custom-tailoring it. Rewrite the cover letter to meet the needs and expectations of the specific employer you're sending it to.

· ·

Your job search is entering its active phase, and whether or not you are currently working becomes a factor. If you're unemployed, you'll want to install an answering machine at home that's separate from the one your family uses. And you'll also want to announce to the world that you're out there job hunting.

But if you're currently employed, you must proceed with caution. My advice is to tell no one at the office of your plans to move on. Never do your job search on company time. Plan interviews early in the morning, at lunchtime or late at night. One job seeker told me he flew from Indiana to New York and back in one evening for a job interview—and made it. Potential employers, he said, are fairly considerate about these matters. And he got the job.

You have to keep your job search on the q.t., because if your present boss finds out you're hunting for a job, you may be fired immediately. Employers demand absolute loyalty.

If you're holding down a job, get an answering machine for your home and give out that number only. Getting calls at the workplace is something your current boss will hate, and doing so may jeopardize your chances for a good reference. And even if you sneak around successfully and your boss never knows you're job hunting on company time, your potential employers will know. They also view it as unprofessional and threatening and will judge you for being so reckless.

· · · · · · · · · · · · · · · · *Coach's Tip* · · · · · · · · · · · · · · · ·

Don't flood the market with your resume. It's counterproductive. Never send out more than five at a time to specifically targeted companies. If you hear back from all five—a happy thought—you'll be frustrated to discover you won't be able to respond as immediately or as well as you want to.

· ·

However, if scores of classified ads interest you, apply for as many as you want. You're less likely to hear back from each of them because of the number of other people also applying.

Your resumes now are out there, working for you. You've done your homework and set up an agenda for responding to nibbles from employers. Now let the interviews begin.

4

Landing the Job

Making actual connections with real jobs and real employers, sending out resumes, doing more research, preparing for the job interview and following up on it while continuing to hunt elsewhere—that could be the description of a full-time job in itself. A *very* full-time job.

················ *Coach's Tip* ················

Treat this facet of landing the right job as a 9 to 5, five-days-a-week assignment at least, even if you already have a full-time job. Schedule your time carefully, and keep a record of everything you do and of everything that needs to be done.

Start sending your resume to the companies and agencies you've researched in the for-profit, nonprofit and governmental sectors of the labor market. Even though your best bet is to apply at smaller companies, send your job applications to the larger firms, too, if they appeal to you. Even as the Fortune 500 companies continue to downsize, they also continue to hire, albeit in smaller numbers and often at lower salaries. In 1993, some two million net new jobs were created, despite the thousands of layoffs.

To meet the demanding task of job hunting, one ambitious job seeker, a recent MBA graduate who had her eye on the largest firms, did her homework and selected the ten companies she most wanted to work for, even though she had not seen one job advertised in her field of financial services and the data she had collected on these firms indicated they were not in a hiring mode. Nonetheless, she used the marketing skills she learned in graduate school to market herself and obtain those precious job interviews that can possibly lead to jobs. With the seriousness that job hunting today requires, she made a chart of the companies, her schedule for contacting each, her contact person, telephone numbers, financial background and target dates for each job application.

She kept the chart next to her bed, so it was the first thing she saw in the morning and the last thing at night. There, in front of her eyes, was her job strategy. "I forced myself to go down the list of company after company, first calling my contacts, then sending an individualized resume and then following up with a request for a personal interview," she told me. "It was tough to do because I needed a job so badly—I have a lot of college debts to pay off—and I wanted to get started on my career. I followed my schedule every single day, and that gave me a much-needed sense of accomplishment."

Her diligence paid off. She didn't have to go any further than the fifth company she had targeted. Though she got no responses from her first two choices—she said she likes to think they simply weren't hiring—her third, fourth and fifth choices were interested enough to talk to her in person. And the fifth choice offered her a job at the first interview.

· · · · · · · · · · · · · · · · · *Coach's Tip* · · · · · · · · · · · · · · · ·

Organize your job search so you won't be overwhelmed, can proceed systematically and can see what you've accomplished. The feeling that you're actually moving things along gives you an extra push to keep on keeping on.

· ·

If you're currently employed, you have an even harder assignment to line up those coveted job interviews because you have less time to search and also must keep secret your urge to work someplace else—unless your employer has told you that your job is gone and gives you permission to look on company time.

··············· *Coach's Tip* ···············

Don't quit your job to job hunt unless you absolutely can't stand your present job for another day. In that case it's better for your mental health to get out alive. But having a job gives you a strong sense of security while hunting elsewhere—plus money to live on. Your present job is your showcase, and you've earned it.

···

Make clear in all communications with a potential employer, both oral and written, that you're currently working and everything must be kept confidential until a job offer is made. Don't let anyone contact your present employer until the new job is secure because you may find yourself out of a job. Give as references colleagues you trust, former employers and other people outside of the office who know and respect your work. If you use co-workers, ask if you can list their home phone numbers for extra protection.

··············· *Coach's Tip* ···············

Don't answer blind ads. One may be from your employer, and then there will be two job openings at your firm instead of one.

···

If you're currently employed, use early mornings, lunch hours, evenings, weekends, holidays and vacation time to job hunt. But be sure to keep up your usual high quality of work. Jack Erdlen, president of Strategic Outsourcing in Boston and a veteran human resource professional, urges job seekers not to "feel guilty about being sneaky, dishonest or disloyal toward your employer. Remember your alternatives: You can stay with the firm and be unhappy and risk termination, or quit and face the professional and financial consequences. As distasteful as it may seem, changing jobs is a fact of life."

················ *Coach's Tip* ················

If you're changing jobs while currently employed, do it as if you were a porcupine making love: very carefully.
···

Job hunting in the city in which you reside is fairly easy to handle whether or not you're employed. But since mobility is such an important factor in a global marketplace—which also might be a good way to describe moving from Philadelphia, for instance, to Los Angeles!—you need to budget money and time for interviews with companies that are out of town.

················ *Coach's Tip* ················

If you're unemployed, you may need to take a part-time or temporary job to finance your job search. If you're employed, you will have to schedule trips carefully to coincide with your free time.
···

I get a lot of mail from people who are planning to move soon or simply want to live and work somewhere else. They wonder what they should do first, move or get a job. I advise them, if it's financially feasible, to wait till they actually make the move to their new location and have more of a feel for the community and the local job market. Of course, if they know of job openings in advance, they should apply immediately. Just remember, I tell them, that no matter how wonderful you are, few employers will keep a job open for you until you get there, and many are cutting down on paying the costs of relocation.

················· *Coach's Tip* ·················

When you send out your resumes, you may want to send them by certified mail so you know they've been received. I've also found that slightly more sophisticated mailings— but not telegrams—are noted by personnel staff as an indication that you are very professional and serious about getting the job. Knowing the date your resume arrived also gives you a good idea of when to start calling for an appointment.

No matter how excellent your resume and cover letter are, if a company did not request to see it, you probably won't get a call back to come in for an interview. That's why it's up to you to keep the process going. After sending out your resume, call in a few days to see if it has been received. Be polite, and don't press too hard to get an answer. Not at this point, because what is important is getting the job interview, which can lead to a job. Ideally, you'd like to hear that yes, your resume was received, it's impressive and they want to meet you right away. More often the only answer you'll get may be an abrupt yes, but be gracious because now you have the information you need to plan your next move.

Unless you've had some previous contact with the company, I'd wait one week before calling back to request an interview. If you're lucky, you may even get a call before you call them.

················· *Coach's Tip* ·················

If you're answering a blind ad, with no company name given, all you can do is send your resume and continue your vigorous job hunt. There is no way you can personally follow up.

You may have to call at least three times before you get through to the interviewer; if you can't get through by then, go on to your next lead. When you do get through, be brief and to the point. Ask when you may come in for an interview. Once again,

I'd limit myself to three phone calls, and then forget it. There's no way to force someone to see you who doesn't want to.

················· *Coach's Tip* ················

If you have to, communicate through the interviewer's secretary or voice mail. Leave messages saying that you are available to come in at any time (even if that's not true). Say you'll call back for an answer, or ask that one be left on your machine. Don't leave anything to chance.

···

When you get the invitation from a prospective employer, set the date for the interview as soon as possible; after all, you don't want to take the chance that someone else will be hired before you even get your foot in the door. But the job interview probably will not be the very next day, and even with only 24 hours, that gives you enough time for the next important step.

Now is the time to hit the books again, this time to update your information about the company where you'll be interviewing. Even though you may have done intensive research only a month or two ago, a lot can change in that time. Perhaps the company has a new owner. Perhaps it's expanding into a new market. Maybe it's shutting down some of its branches. You need to know all of this up front, not just because the information is important to you but also so that you can show how intelligent and thorough you are at the job interview. It will be impressive during the interview when you say, "I hear you've just acquired the Big Widget Company for $3 million. Is that the division you're hiring for?"

················· *Coach's Tip* ················

While you're checking out the latest financial statements and business reports, it won't hurt to find out what you can about the company's benefits. If you're especially concerned about family and work issues, see if the company has been included in newspaper or magazine articles about good family-oriented programs.

···

You may be surprised to learn that the most family-oriented industries are chemicals and publishing, according to a survey by the Partnership Group, a national consulting firm in Lansdale, Pennsylvania. Most people don't equate the manufacturing industry with family concerns, but the industry does have them, possibly because they are more unionized than service industries. Insurance, paper and banking organizations ranked second; health care and financial services, third; aerospace, retail, scientific equipment and electronics, fourth; and wholesale and commodities, last.

·················· *Coach's Tip* ··················

You can't rule out a possible job opportunity because the company isn't active in the area of family concerns—yet. But it is important to know what to expect in case questions about family responsibilities come up in the interview.

··

Realistically, one of the things you'll have on your mind in advance of the interview—in addition to worrying about what you'll say and what kind of impression you'll make—is what your actual chances are of getting the job. Women and minorities, long the victims of discrimination in hiring, are particularly concerned.

·················· *Coach's Tip* ··················

If you are skilled, qualified and fit into the corporate culture, your chances of being hired are good.

··

The demographics projected for this decade and well into the 21st century by the U.S. Department of Labor suggest a radically changing workforce. Only 15 percent of net new hires in the 1990s will be white men, a figure that reflects a dearth of workers ages 16 to 25, the typical entry-level years. White men still will be in demand and probably still preferred, despite antidiscrimination laws. But there won't be enough of them to hire, and that means employers will have to interview all qualified job candidates, regardless of gender, race, religion, ethnic background, age or disabilities. And not only interview a diversified pool of applicants but actually hire them.

················ *Coach's Tip* ················

These projections about the makeup of the workforce are the reasons you've been hearing so often the words *diversity, diverse workforce* and *new diversity.* They are important facts of life in today's labor force.

··

You now have all the information you can possibly acquire, but there's more to a job interview than knowing the important data. You also must make a good impression. As superficial as it may be even to talk about your appearance, it's the first thing an interviewer notices, even before you open your mouth.

················ *Coach's Tip* ················

Even if the office atmosphere is informal and employees are allowed to wear jeans and T-shirts or warm-up suits, you are not an employee. You want to be one.

··

If you're a woman, wear a business suit; it shows you mean business. I know women who were not hired because they wore a pantsuit to the interview. That bothers me because it reeks of sexism, but if you want the job, it's important to know that pantsuits or even too-short skirts may work against you. After you get the job, you can challenge these Neanderthal attitudes, but right now you want the job.

If you're a man, wear a suit and tie, or a jacket and tie. Be well groomed. Interviewers worry that if you appear "sloppy" at a job interview, how would you dress if you got the job?

I feel from talking to human resource personnel that they take casual dress personally, as if what you are wearing is a slap in their face, disrespectful to them. I am constantly surprised when seemingly casual, easygoing executives tell me, with no apologies, that when they interview people, they want them to be well dressed, their hair neat, their shoes shined. It absolutely matters to them, and they are the ones who matter.

················ *Coach's Tip* ················

Though the dress codes and implicit conformity required may make you feel somewhat uncomfortable, pay great attention to your appearance on a job interview—and you can bet that the interviewer will be doing the same.

··

Arrive at the interview at least 15 minutes early, and wait patiently. Observe your surroundings and see what you can soak up about the corporate culture, how employees behave and if the atmosphere seems relaxed or strictly disciplined. This is important information because it is *your* first impression.

················ *Coach's Tip* ················

Often, even before you have an interview with a living, human being, you may be asked to take an aptitude or skills test. Don't be nervous; just do the best you can. Asking you to take the tests is a good sign because it means the employer is serious about you and about filling the position.

··

Taking a psychological test, however, is a different matter, and one you have to think about first. A preemployment psychological test can be grounds for a discrimination-in-hiring lawsuit, especially if it includes questions about religion, personal habits, sexual orientation or political opinions. I get frequent calls from anguished job seekers who don't want to take the test but do want to get the job. They tell me they often feel the real test is to see whether or not they'll take the test, and the results probably aren't even noted. I wouldn't bet on that, although it's true the job applicant never gets any feedback on the outcome of the psychological portion of the test, and those who refuse to take them usually are out of the running.

To me, a psychological test is as offensive and should be as illegal as is the use of lie detectors in the workplace. They certainly don't help anyone get a job; they certainly do screen out "undesirables." Psychological tests are such a touchy matter with employers that I wouldn't even ask if they were mandatory.

· · · · · · · · · · · · · · · · · *Coach's Tip* · · · · · · · · · · · · · · · · ·

It's probably best to take a psychological test if it's a job you really want. I would be careful in my answers, however, to try to beat the test by answering exactly what you know they want to hear. For instance, if they ask you whether you believe in the free enterprise system, I would immediately say yes. And if they ask you whether you would ever consider joining a union, you know what the answer is: "Perish the thought!"

· ·

If you feel the test is discriminatory, after the interview write down the questions that you believe are illegal. If you don't get the job, you may have grounds for a discrimination lawsuit—and several have been won on these grounds. But that's not the same as getting a job.

Preemployment screening and testing must be endured, and hopefully you'll be able to ace them. But the long-awaited, actual job interview itself—there you must be proactive and not solely reactive.

Now that I have you all tensed up about the job interview, relax. You have plenty to offer, or you wouldn't be asked to come in for an interview. Remember, too, that a job is open and the company needs to fill it. Why not with you?

One of my favorite corporate vice presidents of human resources—and I admit he's not typical—tells me that "one of the things an applicant would hardly ever think about is that the interviewer is as scared as the job seeker. If I fit the right person to the right job, it's nothing extraordinary. But if the wrong person is hired, then everyone notices that."

················ *Coach's Tip* ················

You know you're well qualified, well informed about the company and perfectly dressed, so smile and exude tremendous confidence. Without being arrogant, think how lucky this company is to meet you—that should make you smile. . . . !

··

If you're being interviewed in someone's private office and in most cases, you will be—look around for something to make a personal connection with. Fitting into the corporate culture, which means having similar values and goals, will be an important factor in whether or not you get a job offer.

Casual conversation is okay for openers, and it's also okay for you to be the first to talk. You can mention how excited you are to be there and how eager you are to work for the company; but if you see displayed a family photo or a sports trophy or a humorous slogan, comment on that, too, stressing what you have in common.

················ *Coach's Tip* ················

Though you are relaxed and warm and wonderful, don't talk too much.

··

A personnel interviewer told me that he was ready to hire a job applicant "but he wouldn't shut up long enough for me to tell him he was hired. The longer he talked, the less I liked him. He talked himself out of the job."

Answer all questions briefly and seriously, though your asides and other comments certainly can be humorous. And humor helps break the ice when an interviewer is icily formal. Most first interviews last no longer than 20 minutes.

It doesn't happen often, but because I've received several calls about the problem, you must know in advance that some interviewers are obsessed with their own power and victimize job hunters by playing games. Their questions have nothing to do with performing the job well; they're usually about your favorite movie, book, TV show, sports team, restaurant or political candidate.

·················· *Coach's Tip* ················

You must answer questions from left field that make you feel uncomfortable—perhaps that's the point of them—but you don't have to answer them honestly. And you can turn such questions around to work in your favor, to show how quick you are and that it's not easy to intimidate you.

··

Arlene S. Hirsch, a career counselor, says a job candidate for a managerial job was asked, "If you were stranded on a desert island and could have only one person with you, who would it be?" The candidate's resourceful reply: "A boat builder." She says that another client was asked, "What kind of animal would you like to be?" The reply: "What kind of animal do you like to hire?" The client got the job.

At some point in the interview, either at the beginning or very end, the company's representative probably will ask if you want to say anything about yourself—short of your life story. This is the time to showcase your personality, charm and intrinsic good nature.

·················· *Coach's Tip* ················

While your monologue will be carefully noted and you will be judged for what you want to be known about yourself, what really is being tested here is your ability to communicate, relax, converse and get along with other people.

··

It's fine to talk about your childhood, where you grew up and how you became interested in your present work and to give insights into your values and ethics, but once again, keep it short. And do it all with a smile.

While you want to answer every question truthfully and completely, you should not answer certain questions at all in the preemployment interview: queries about your age, race, ethnic background, sexual orientation, religious beliefs or disabilities.

·················· *Coach's Tip* ················

If interviewers ask what clearly is an offensive question, remain calm. Do not become confrontational. Do not accuse them of violating federal, state and local antidiscrimination laws (which they probably are).

··

Instead, try to address the question head-on. If it's about age, you might reply that chronological years don't matter when someone's as healthy and fit as you are. (This may not be true; but since you're being forced to reply to an illegal question, you're entitled to give whatever answer you want and remedy it later when you have the job.)

Women, in particular, report they are asked innumerable questions about their family responsibilities, despite Title 7 of the 1964 U.S. Civil Rights Act that prohibits sex discrimination in hiring. Typical questions are about the size of your family, if you plan to have more children, whether you are available to travel, what kind of child-care arrangements you have, what you would do if your husband were transferred or what you would do if a child got sick and you had to be at work.

Those questions aren't subtle, but women tell me they've been asked ones that are even more blunt, such as the following: "What kind of birth control do you take?" "Would you quit your job if you had a baby?" "Do you believe in abortion?" "Would your husband allow you to go out of town on business with a male colleague?"

Some of these nasty questions might be legitimate once you are hired, when more detailed personal questions are allowed for your supervisor's information, for employment records and benefits. But not now.

·················· *Coach's Tip* ················

For now, the best way to handle these illegitimate questions is to reply as follows, in a calm voice and with a pleasant smile: "I am an extremely responsible adult, and no employer has ever had to worry that I will not fulfill every single job obligation I have. In fact, I'm known for my conscientious work and loyalty. I never leave anyone in the lurch." And then change the subject.

··

This may come as a surprise, but most human resource executives consider a job interview as a two-way street: they ask you questions and you ask them questions. In fact, most interviewers say they judge job applicants by the questions they ask as well as the questions they answer.

·················· *Coach's Tip* ················

Ask questions about the company and your future in it, but try to avoid asking questions about personal matters—your own or the company's.

··

You'll want to know, and you'll get points for asking questions such as these: How many people are in my department? To whom would I report? What kind of career path would I be on? What would be my next step up? Would I be eligible for any training programs? Do you have performance reviews? Why do you (the interviewer) so obviously enjoy working for this company?

If you feel extremely comfortable with the interviewer, you might want to ask why this particular job is open. Is it a newly created job? Or will you be filling a vacancy? And if the interviewer seems to be willing to answer any question you ask, the next good query is, why did the previous person leave? The answer to the latter probably will be the most helpful information you can glean from the interview.

As uncomfortable as it may make you—and the interviewer—for your own protection you must ask about the financial condition of the company. The interviewer will expect this question from a savvy job applicant who wants to avoid having to job search all over again in a few months. Even the most top-ranking executives forget to do this basic homework duty, and the time to do it is at the job interview, when corporations can be held legally responsible for lying about the status of the company. Many new employees, suddenly back on the job market, have collected large sums of money for damages for lack of full disclosure.

Learn a lesson from John Sculley, former head of Apple Computer and an executive much in demand. In 1993, he took a job as head of Spectrum Information Technologies, which looked like an important move. But a few months later, he resigned after learning about a Securities and Exchange Commission probe of the firm and some accounting "problems." If Sculley, in all his wisdom, had asked the right questions up front, he would have avoided an embarrassing and devastating job experience. To his chagrin, he learned the importance of full disclosure.

· · · · · · · · · · · · · · · · *Coach's Tip* · · · · · · · · · · · · · · · ·

Do all the research in advance about the company that you can, but during the job interview, don't forget to pop the question, "How's the company doing?" And remember, the company is legally responsible for its answers.

· ·

Here are some questions *not* to ask during the interview:

- How many weeks vacation will I get?

- Are personal phone calls okay?

- How much time do I get for lunch?

- Is the CEO a hands-on kind of person or mostly invisible?

- Do you have a job for my cousin?

- Can I have time off instead of overtime pay?

While they have you there in their offices, some employers try to get a little more out of you than the job interview demands. It's perfectly ethical for them to ask to see samples of your work, if it's appropriate, or to ask your opinion about particular job situations or your expert advice on pertinent financial matters.

If you're a graphic artist, for instance, asking to see your work is similar to reading your resume and cover letter. But watch out for several gray areas regarding potential employers asking for examples of your work; you should try to avoid them. One man, an African American, told me that when he applied for a drafting job, he was asked to show his facility at using CAD/CAM computer programs. He was told the "practice" session was to make sure each job applicant was treated fairly and equally. He did the work, which took several hours, did not get the job and was later told by an employee that his work had been used by the company and billed to the client. "This was all in the name of equal opportunity," he said.

"And what did the office look like?" I asked him. "Despite its possible unethical practices, is the firm an equal opportunity employer?" He replied, "The day I was there, I saw only white men."

·················· *Coach's Tip* ··················

Try to protect yourself by asking up front if the sample work you do actually will be used. Then you can make your decision about whether it's worthwhile to pursue the job.

··

An experienced freelance marketing expert was asked to create a marketing plan when she applied for a full-time job. It took her one week to do it. Her work was not acknowledged; she was not offered the job. In retribution she sent the company a bill for her hours of service and added, in a postscript, that she had a brother who breaks people's legs when they don't pay their bills. "I don't have a brother," she told me cheerily.

As difficult as one job interview is, you may have several before getting a job offer. Because there is an emphasis on team-work, you may be interviewed not only by the hiring executive but also by several members of the team, who will come to a consensus about whether to hire you.

···············   *Coach's Tip*   ···············

At the end of your interview shake hands, say you hope to hear from them soon and then ask—once again, with a smile—"Well, how am I doing?" When you get home—and you will—write a note thanking the interviewer, saying that you hope to hear good news soon and that you will be calling shortly.

···

The question about how you're doing doesn't necessarily in-dicate insecurity. It means you want to know. Psychologically, it lines up the interviewer on your side. And you may even get some helpful suggestions.

It also brings you one step closer to the job offer.

·····5·····

The Job Offer

 After a series of job interviews—and they may go on for months—it's time to start thinking about what you will do when you get the job offer. However, even a series of interviews, no matter how thorough and exhaustive they may be, do not guarantee that a job offer ever will be made. One of the most important steps in your self-marketing is to get over this hurdle and get the job offer you so richly deserve. As with everything else in accelerating your job search, you also will have to make the job offer happen.

With your usual professional calm and diplomacy, you should be able to handle any stumbling block to achieving your goal. One of the most difficult, because something is intrinsically insulting about it, is to be told that you are very close to being hired but that the company is concerned that you are overqualified for the job.

Overqualified is a buzzword that only occasionally means what it says. The adjective usually is used to cover the company's concern that the job, which they perceive as a boring one, may bore you. Or it could mean that the hiring officer respects your skills and education but doesn't want to pay you for them. And mature job seekers tell me that when they hear "overqualified," they know right away, rightly or wrongly, that they're being rejected because of their age.

··················· *Coach's Tip* ··················

When you hear hesitancy in an interviewer's voice about your so-called plethora of skills, deal with it at face value and turn it into another opportunity to sell yourself.
··

A 38-year-old man with ten years of experience in one field was told he was overqualified when he applied for an entry-level job in a new field he wanted to switch to. Since he clearly wasn't overqualified, he understood that the company was concerned he was too mature for a beginner's job, had been making a slightly higher salary and might be difficult to manage, especially since his manager was 27 years old.

The job applicant told me he almost panicked when he heard the word *overqualified*, because up to that point he knew he had done well in the interviews and thought he had the job. But he quickly pulled himself together and said to the interviewer, "I know I have a lot of experience and skills, and I'm proud of them because they add to what I bring to this job. I not only take orders well; I'm also a team player, and if I can share my knowledge with others, I'll be happy to do so. And I hope they'll share their knowledge with me, because, after all, no matter what I've previously done, here I'm the new kid on the block and I'll need all the help I can get."

His answer, which accurately described his situation, soothed the fears of the interviewer—and he got the job. One year later, he reported that he's doing well. Though he helps his co-workers in some areas of their responsibilities, he receives much more assistance than he gives. "I certainly am not overqualified," he said, "though sometimes I wish I actually were."

Job interviews that spread out over several months are another hurdle to leap because they sap your strength and confidence. But employers, who are in the catbird seat in a capricious labor market, are taking their time in sorting through job candidates.

A new college graduate I know had 14 interviews with an international consulting firm. She was told at her first interview that 19 others were being considered for the job, an overwhelming piece of information.

One month later, at her second interview, she was told the field had been narrowed to ten. At each interview, the number of job candidates diminished, and the questioning became more intense. Finally, six months later, she was informed that she was one of two candidates being considered, and she got the job.

She was told her professional attitude while waiting for the job offer was a key factor in her being hired over the others, who did not handle the uncertainty as well as she did. But that was only her outer demeanor. Inside, she says she was a wreck. "After that long period of time, I would have been devastated if I had been eliminated," she said. "I don't know who the other candidates were because they never let us meet each other, but I certainly feel sorry for them."

················ *Coach's Tip* ················

It's understandable for you to be sorry for yourself and others who do not get a job offer, but don't let turndowns be turnoffs.

··

It's not unrealistic to look at a turndown this way. In baseball the odds are against getting a hit. The same is true with a job offer: If it doesn't work out, you can say you struck out and now can start again. The next time the percentages are higher that you'll get a hit.

People in sales have a strong mental attitude when it comes to rejection—and they'd better have one. Their attitude is that you get 100 turndowns before you get a yes. So when the turndown comes, it's one more out of the way, and you're that much closer to an acceptance.

················· *Coach's Tip* ·················

Don't put all your eggs in one basket. No matter how rosy your chances look to get the job, don't rest on your laurels. Keep looking. Keep on plugging. Line up every job opportunity you can until you have a job offer in hand, just in case it never comes.

··

Another serious problem arises when your former employers or other references give you a bad reference. Often you have no idea that you're being bad-mouthed or that it's the reason you aren't getting any job offers.

Former employers must be very careful what they say about you, or you can take them to court and sue for damages. But how do you find out what they're saying?

After a series of otherwise unexplainable terminations of job interviews without a job offer, be suspicious that your references are the problem. The job interviewer probably won't tell you they are, but you could ask anyway.

················· *Coach's Tip* ·················

One way to find out what your former boss is saying is to contact Documented Reference Check, a national agency that finds out for you 800-742-3316; the fee is about $60.

··

Some job seekers must knock down another barrier when it arises, namely, the interviewer's question, "Why have you changed jobs so often?" Or, "Why have you had so many different jobs?" Human resource personnel frankly tell me they are concerned about people who do what they call "job-hop." I was on a television show recently with an employer from an international manufacturing firm. He said out loud, for everyone to hear, that he was "leery" of people who have too many jobs on their resume, no matter the cause.

Though his comment doesn't sound fair in view of the corporate downsizings and layoffs that are endemic in the U.S. labor market, he was telling the truth. And knowing the truth helps us deal with the problem.

If you've had different jobs every two or three years, you've listed each one on your resume and you're *still* called in for a job interview, you know that the company is interested in you and that you are operating from a base of power, small power, but still one with some leverage.

· · · · · · · · · · · · · · · · *Coach's Tip* · · · · · · · · · · · · · · · ·

Explain what happened to each job. Start by saying, "It looks as if I'm a job-hopper, but I'm not. What I want more than anything else is to become an integral part of your company—and a long-term employee."

· ·

If the changes were due to layoffs, say so. Everyone understands that today. If your job was replaced by a smart machine, they understand that, too. If the company went bankrupt, that's also a familiar scenario.

However, if there were personality differences or you were discharged for poor performance, I wouldn't be so completely forthcoming as to reveal those reasons. They may or not come out in a reference check, so I wouldn't be the first to bring them up. I would simply say things didn't work out and how sorry you were they didn't. Say that you learned a lot from the experience and have become a far more valuable employee because of it. Then leave the ball in their court.

If you changed jobs frequently early on in your career, it probably is the truth if you explain you were trying to find the right job, the right career—and that now, after a lot of hard work and training, you have done so.

················· *Coach's Tip* ·················

If you did job-hop because you were young and inexpe-
rienced, I would say so, explaining, "I was immature then,
but I've grown up since then and am a professional, de-
pendable worker."
···

You've answered the hard questions, your references check
out, you have shown you will fit in with the company's culture,
you have shown up for every job interview promptly and have
handled the long process maturely. Now you can't do anything
else except wait for the job offer.

················· *Coach's Tip* ·················

If, at the end of what you presumed was your last interview, no job offer was made, you have the right to ask if
you can expect one. And if so, when?
···

If you don't get one within a week, call to ask what is happening. If you can't get through for an answer, it may not be a
negative sign; it may mean only that other people are being interviewed. Call again in another week. Ask for a progress report.
Do this for one month, and if you still receive no response, forget
about the job. During this time you were continuing your other
job searches anyway, so it wasn't a total loss.

················· *Coach's Tip* ·················

You may feel terribly disappointed that no job offer was
made after all those months of interviewing and anxiety,
but many people tell me they get a call with a job offer as
much as six months after their last interview. As I've noted
before, most companies take their time.
···

But when some companies find exactly the right candidate, they want to bring their job search process to a close as quickly as possible. And when you do get the job offer—that means the interviewer says those beautiful words, "We want you to work for us!"—your job-hunting ordeal may be over.

You finally have the job offer, but you don't quite have the job yet. There are a few other matters to clear up in advance, and the most important of these is salary. You may have noticed that I haven't previously mentioned how to deal with salary in a job interview. That's because you should not deal with salary at this juncture, unless you feel you will be eliminated from consideration if you don't give a salary range. If you're asked what you expect to make in advance of a job offer and you feel you can delay answering, your best reply, to avoid eliminating yourself from the running, is to say, "I'll be glad to discuss salary with you once you offer me the job. However, I am extremely flexible on the subject."

· · · · · · · · · · · · · · · · *Coach's Tip* · · · · · · · · · · · · · · · ·

Cross your fingers when you say "flexible." You want to be paid fairly and want to get as much money as you can.
· ·

Negotiating a salary is difficult in a tight labor market because you don't have a lot of leverage—i.e., scores of other job opportunities. But by now you know the company wants you to fill the job, and that does give you a base from which to work.

· · · · · · · · · · · · · · · · *Coach's Tip* · · · · · · · · · · · · · · · ·

Knowledge is power, and that means finding out all you can about what your job's salary range is. It's not likely you'll be able to go beyond that range, but you want to start somewhere in the middle, rather than at the bottom.
· ·

Your first question in the salary negotiation is to ask for a job description. If it doesn't list the job category and the salary range, ask if the company has job categories and if so, what yours is. Ask directly what the salary or the salary range is. When you get this information, you know what you have to work with.

Your previous research, of course, has given you some idea of the salary, even if the interviewer never mentioned it. Finding out what a company pays is extremely difficult, unless the company is unionized. Otherwise, employers keep salaries completely secret; some even threaten to fire employees who discuss the subject with anyone at all.

· · · · · · · · · · · · · · · · · *Coach's Tip* · · · · · · · · · · · · · · · · ·

Check salaries in your area of expertise through professional associations or trade groups, research them at the library or call your local office of the U.S. Bureau of Labor Statistics; ask friends in the field what they earn or what their salary range is; ask anyone you know working at the company you're interviewing with if they can give you a handle on what the job pays. Above all, be discreet.

· ·

The Catch-22 is that employers like to think you want to work for them because they are such wonderful people, which they might be. If you make too much noise about what your pay will be, they might suspect your only interest is making money. And that, ironically—because it's their motive, too—turns them off.

· · · · · · · · · · · · · · · · · *Coach's Tip* · · · · · · · · · · · · · · · · ·

Listed at the end of this book are up-to-date salary figures for what I consider the 100 best jobs for the 1990s and beyond. Hopefully, the job you're offered is among them. If it isn't, perhaps one of the 100 best is in the same field as yours. In that case its salary may be a clue to help ascertain what you should be making.

· ·

················ *Coach's Tip* ················

If you are offered a salary you think is fair, one that falls within the parameters of what the job pays, your skills, experience and future responsibilities—take it. This is no time to play games.
··

But based on your research, if the offer is far below your expectations, you must negotiate a better one. While operating from the position that the company is extremely interested in you, make a counteroffer, one that is fairly close to the one you actually want. Show the hiring officer the data you have collected about salaries for this specific job. I think he or she will be impressed and far more willing to make a deal.

················ *Coach's Tip* ················

Remember, this is a negotiation, not a fight. Don't be confrontational or outraged. State the facts simply and unemotionally.
··

If the company isn't willing to bend on their initial offer, you have the choice of turning down the job. But that's probably not what you want to do, unless you feel the offer is too outrageous to live with.

If this is a full-time job—and hopefully it is—consider benefits as part of the salary. This is an accurate way to figure out your compensation package, because if you have to pay for health care, college tuition, child care or insurance on your own, you will quickly realize that they involve real money.

················ *Coach's Tip* ················

If the salary really grates on you but you realize the offer is a very firm one—and you want the job—agree to it graciously. Then ask for a salary review in six months to discuss it again.
··

You will be granted that opportunity, I'm certain, and in that time period you'll have a better chance to find out what your colleagues are earning and prove your worth to the company. After six months on the job, you'll be able to argue your case more forcefully and effectively.

Company benefits must be distributed uniformly among all employees, regardless of job title, as mandated by the federal government. But so-called perks are given solely on the whim of the employer. Perks include a company car, free parking, club membership, training programs, committee assignments, office space and support staff.

•••••••••••••••• *Coach's Tip* ••••••••••••••••

Part of your negotiating includes asking about perks. If you're not offered ones you think you should have, ask if you're eligible for them. Getting perks directly affects your own bottom line. Don't be shy about asking. Now is the time.

••

Relocation also is a factor that you must take into account before your final handshake. While some people are thrilled to start a new job in a new locale, the move is often hard to make if you have a spouse and family. Many questions—most of them involving money—have to be worked out in advance. Otherwise the move could be a nightmare, and the job will not work out.

If you have to relocate, ask everything you can think of about expenses and other potential problems. Here are some examples:

- Ask about reimbursement for trips to look at your new location before making an actual move as well as trips by your spouse or other family members.

- Ask about reimbursement for the costs of moving.

- What about daycare assistance, if necessary?

- Do you need career counseling for your spouse?

- Don't forget to ask about who carries the cost of your present home if it doesn't sell right away.

- Who pays the cost of your living in a hotel or motel until your new place to live is ready or a new house is purchased?

- If the REALTOR® doesn't seem to know about the school system, will you be reimbursed for getting consultation on the best school for your children?

- And who pays for transporting your car if the new location is too far away?

·················· *Coach's Tip* ··················

Make a list of questions about relocation, and be sure to ask each of them. The questions probably won't be resolved at your final job interview, but make certain you have every concern out on the table.
··

Once you pass your medical exam, you may find that your firm wants you and every employee—at every level—to sign an employment contract when they join the company. These contracts are written to ensure that you keep the company's financial information confidential. In addition, the company will want to ensure that as an employee, you are not competing with their business in your free time. If you are asked to sign an employment contract, go over it very carefully because it will affect your future. If you leave the company, you may be limited in where you can work and what you can do.

·················· *Coach's Tip* ··················

Don't sign an employment contract without consulting a lawyer. But remember, if you want the job, you will have to sign it.
··

Now you are set to start your new job—almost. For your own protection you must get a written employment agreement or letter from your employer. A written agreement delineates your reponsibilities, hours, salary, benefits, whom you report to, when you are expected to start, vacation time and other details you've discussed. An employment agreement protects you legally if you show up for work on the appointed date and find you have no job—or that someone else has been hired instead. It also clearly spells out what is expected of you.

If you're currently employed, ask for at least two weeks to give notice and help train someone else to do your job before starting the new one. That's the professional thing to do, and your new employer will respect you for it. And when you do give notice, be as pleasant as possible. No recriminations. After all, you did get out of there alive, and you still may need a good reference.

·················· *Coach's Tip* ··················

Try to leave as good an impression as possible when you leave your job. Don't burn any bridges.

···

If you're unemployed, it's also a good idea not to start your new job right away. You need some recovery time from the anguish of being unemployed and from the strong feelings of insecurity. Ask for at least two weeks, which is a routine request. It will probably be granted. If they want you to start immediately, take that as a compliment and start immediately.

·················· *Coach's Tip* ··················

Use whatever time you have before starting work to relax, enjoy yourself, make plans and build your confidence.

···

When you start your new job, you want to hit the ground running, and this brief lead time should be devoted to being nice to yourself and also planning how you will handle your new job assignment. Remember, this is what you've been waiting for: the chance to land the right job.

Congratulations, you did it! The next step is to make sure you keep it.

PART TWO

Keeping
Your Job

·····6·····

Keeping Current

 In my daily columns for the *Chicago Tribune*, I often say that I'm "giving advice to the joblorn." But that word doesn't describe you at all, because you either have just started a new job, one you want, or you currently work in one you want to keep.

There's nothing joblorn about that highly desirable state. But you can't rest on your laurels. You have to be proactive and not solely reactive to maintain the nirvana you've attained.

Confidence comes from knowing what's going on, starting with your own office or factory. It comes from doing your homework. I know you thought you were finished doing your homework, and for the most part, you are. You won't have to continue the intensive research that was required to land the job.

However, you will have to keep up to date with what's happening inside your company in particular, in your profession and in the economy. You can achieve this in a variety of ways.

One of the best places to find out what's going on in the world of work that's pertinent to you and your career progress is in the workplace itself. If you're new on the job, I advise spending the first six months carefully looking and closely listening. Be as quiet as a fly on the wall—unless you're female, and then be as quiet as a bra on the wall. (I know Dr. Spock will forgive me for being risqué.) Ask the questions you need to get your job done, but don't be so intense that you drive your colleagues crazy.

· · · · · · · · · · · · · · · · · *Coach's Tip* · · · · · · · · · · · · · · · ·

During your early weeks on a new job, don't feel you have to be an immediate success. You don't, and in most cases you can't.

· ·

Don't try to come up with a plan to save the company within 48 hours of being hired. It most likely won't be appreciated, and it's probably too early for you to make really helpful suggestions.

A newly hired sales representative told me that the first week on the job he thoughtfully explained to the national wholesale company he worked for how it should reassign its territories and redeploy its personnel. "What a mistake that was," he said. "They looked at me like I was crazy."

No one ridiculed him for trying to be helpful, and he didn't lose his job for his audacity, but he hasn't been taken seriously since then. "They actually were pretty nice about it, but three years later, I'm still in the entry-level job I was hired for," he said.

The company, which is prospering, has not implemented his advice to change their basic mode of operations. And it will take him many years to recover what he lost by his early mistake.

· · · · · · · · · · · · · · · · · · *Coach's Tip* · · · · · · · · · · · · · · · · ·

Keep a low profile in the early days of your job. You'll learn much more that way.

· ·

If you've been on the job for a long time and want to keep it, you have work to do, too. You must be alert to what's happening inside the company and how it relates to you. That's an easier task for you because you've been around awhile; now you must attune your ears to pick up what pertains to you.

For new entrants and experienced workers alike, one of the best sources of inside information is the office grapevine, a much-maligned means of communication that you cannot ignore.

· · · · · · · · · · · · · · · · · · *Coach's Tip* · · · · · · · · · · · · · · · · ·

Be part of the office grapevine, but make sure you never are a part of hurting a co-worker by listening to or trans-mitting vicious comments or malicious gossip.

· ·

The grapevine is abused when it's used to knock people, and you don't want to be a part of that because you too easily could be next. Use the grapevine—a powerful, highly accurate, instan-taneous communication tool—to find out who's leaving, who's getting promoted, what new projects are under way, what the financial outlook of the company is, what training seminars are worthwhile and, above all, who has the real power.

· · · · · · · · · · · · · · · · · · *Coach's Tip* · · · · · · · · · · · · · · · · ·

When you have information to transmit that will help others, do it informally, through the office grapevine, but do it verbally. Never put your information in the computer or send it via E-mail, unless you want the whole world to read it. Don't assume your PC guarantees privacy. It doesn't.

· ·

As a new employee—and this applies to long-term employees as well—carefully read every word of your employee handbook. In it you will find that the company has carefully described all aspects of employment, including hiring and firing.

················· *Coach's Tip* ·················

Read the employee handbook as if it were a bible. It is.
··

The employee handbook was written by the human resources department, but I assure you every word in it was approved by a high-powered employment lawyer. The handbook doesn't constitute a legal contract between you and your employer, but its contents are a strong legal defense for the employer in case you decide to sue.

In addition to knowing the written rules of work, you also need to learn the unwritten rules as well. Unfortunately, management never tells you about them. According to Gerard R. Egan, professor of organization development and psychology at Loyola University of Chicago, the "new reality" of employment today is created by "a global marketplace, constant change and cutthroat competition."

Even though the "old rules" were never explained to employees, the "new rules" of work must be understood in order to adapt and adjust to a dramatically restructured way of doing business. Egan says that with the old rules, all you had to do was to show up for work every day, do a fairly decent job and "keep your nose clean." No one would dream of firing you, the company would go on forever and some 30 years later you'd retire with dignity and fanfare and get a gold watch.

The "new rules" describe an entirely new ball game in which:

- You must contribute every single day.

- You have to learn that you must work hard all day long and have results you can point to.

- You probably will not stay around for your entire career because it's not good for you or the company.

- You can't take for granted that the firm you work for will be successful, that it will never have financial difficulties and never go bankrupt.

- Instead, you have to prepare yourself for that fact that both your job and the company itself may disappear at any moment.

·············· *Coach's Tip* ················

When the experts tell you that you must be flexible to survive in the workplace of the 1990s and the 21st century, one of the things you have to be flexible about is that the company you now work for, no matter how successful it is, may go under from the pressure of foreign competition.

···

In addition to energy and enthusiasm, which you should show on a daily basis without knocking over everyone around you, as a successful employee you'll also have to possess initiative and the ability to be a self-starter and decide for yourself what needs to be done. Then you must do it!

Part of being current is to be in charge of your career and to understand the many factors at play that directly affect you. Keeping current also means knowing the dynamics of how work actually is done. *Teamwork* isn't just a buzzword; it's a fact of work life precipitated by computer technology and corporate emphasis on quality management.

·············· *Coach's Tip* ················

Managers have learned that in order to achieve Total Quality Management (TQM)—in other words, to get the most work and productivity from each employee and to satisfy customers—teamwork is essential.

···

Employers finally have learned a lesson that any worker could have told them years ago. Employees with hands-on experience doing the job know what shortcuts are needed and what changes should be made to increase the bottom line.

That leads to the concept of teamwork—an old phrase, but this time employers have to mean it. They can't keep talking about how wonderful teamwork is without rewarding you for your team efforts and treating you as a valued, respected member of the team.

••••••••••••••••• *Coach's Tip* ••••••••••••••••

Companies that stress teamwork—and increasingly they do because it pays off so well—can't also allow a military style of command to exist in the workplace.

••

Each participant must be able to contribute with dignity. Otherwise, teamwork is a joke. What this adds up to is a decrease in the number of supervisors who yell at employees and an increase in those who try to enlist everyone's cooperation by not being a "what I say goes" dictator or general. (See Chapter 8.)

••••••••••••••••• *Coach's Tip* ••••••••••••••••

If you're not used to working with a team, look at it as a very positive evolution in the workplace. Cooperation often is far more productive than competition.

••

Consider the team of people you work with as your own personal support group, and look at yourself as someone who always will be there for them. You already know you will have to get along with your supervisors. Now you'll have to get along with your team members, too.

Another dramatic change in how most businesses work today is how your work is evaluated. In today's workforce as in the past, you are ultimately judged on your individual accomplishments. But what is relatively new is that before you can achieve recognition for your own work, your team's success will be evaluated, and you will be judged in that framework.

·················· *Coach's Tip* ·················

Because you're part of the team, the other team members have a vested interest in your success because their success depends on your doing well. They will be eager and willing to help you learn the ropes.

··

A few years ago an employee at an auto plant called me to ask why I write so much about teamwork. "We've been doing it forever," he said. "That's how cars are made." But he called again more recently to discuss the subject again and, this time, to tell me about his daughter, an accountant. "She got a good job when she got out of college with a large accounting firm," he told me. "She had learned in school that all accounting firms are made up of cutthroat people, all fighting each other for new accounts. That used to be true."

And that's how she approached her job: as fiercely competitive. She was assigned to a small group of people specializing in handling health-care accounts. "She thought she was doing what she was supposed to do when she tried to outsmart her colleagues and take personal credit for everything the group achieved," her father said. "Before she knew what was happening, she was frozen out of everything the group was doing, got the smallest accounts to work on and nobody talked to her."

When she figured out what she was doing wrong—with the help of some suggestions from her supervisor—she immediately saw the advantages of being a team player. It was the only game in town. "She got smart fast," her father said proudly.

You don't have to go through what this accountant did because you know in advance that if your company stresses teamwork, it's not idle conversation. It's a way of doing business that will become a way of life for you.

Though radical changes are taking place in offices and factories, a few things remain the same, such as being on time and how you look.

· · · · · · · · · · · · · · · · *Coach's Tip* · · · · · · · · · · · · · · · ·

Employers still insist upon well-groomed and punctual
employees.
· ·

I stressed the importance of a neat appearance when I guided
you through the intricacies of the job interview. (See Chapter 4.)
And as patronizing as it sounds because you are savvy adults,
being neatly dressed and well groomed matters on a day-to-day
basis. It matters so much that many people tell me they dress as
if they were in the next job up! Some believe this form of "dress-
ing up" actually helped get them a promotion.

Talking about being on time for work sounds outdated, but
it's something employers mention frequently when I ask them
what they want most from employees. It's a given that you
know how to do the work—or you wouldn't be there—but even
in this day and age employers want you on duty on time, to take
the allotted one hour for lunch and not more, and not to leave
early unless you have a special reason to do so.

· · · · · · · · · · · · · · · · *Coach's Tip* · · · · · · · · · · · · · · · ·

Whether you're starting a new job or have been in the
same one for years, be on time. And if you can't be on time,
explain the situation in advance and give the exact time
you will arrive.
· ·

The boss isn't the only one who's going to notice; your colleagues will, too. And they will be the first to get angry about
your tardiness because they also will be the first ones to have to
pick up the slack your lack of responsibility creates.

A secretary told me with cold disapproval that a colleague—
let's call him John—was always late for work. "Everyone knew
when he finally got here that it was time for us to go to lunch,"
she said. "The only problem was that John went to lunch, too,

ten minutes later. He took a long lunch, strolled back in and then left at 4:30."

Fortunately for John, the little work he did was well done, but the secretary told me he has been warned about his improper work hours and how it affects the productivity of the entire department. John comes in on time now and does a full day's work, she said, "but everyone's still angry at him and watches his comings and goings like hawks." I wouldn't be surprised if it was his colleagues who rightfully complained about him in the first place, thus causing him to get a well-deserved reprimand.

·············· *Coach's Tip* ················

It's not wise to alienate your supervisor. It's sheer folly to aggravate your co-workers.

···

Co-workers know how to get even when they feel abused, especially if they feel underpaid and abused and have to do the work you have neglected to get done. They don't take you out and shoot you, though it may cross their minds; instead, through a swift application of innuendo and rumor, they do you in. And making you the butt of their jokes, as they did with John, gets the word out about your sins even faster.

Office politics, implemented through the use of the office grape-vine (the office communication tool described earlier), were used to get John to pull his full share of the load. It was a power play, because co-workers didn't have the actual leverage to make John do anything. By spreading the word just in case his supervisors had not noticed his behavior, the matter finally came to the ears of someone powerful enough to call John on the carpet.

Through the wheeling and dealing of office politics, people win promotions, snag the best projects and control the behavior of other workers. Office politics is an extremely effective tool, and you cannot afford to ignore it. It can be used to help or to hurt. Hopefully, you'll use it in a positive way—just as you use the office grapevine—to help you build a needed power base in the office rather than to destroy others.

··············· *Coach's Tip* ················

Don't go around saying you're above office politics. Even if you are, you can't afford to be. If you aren't a part of office politics, you'll never keep current on what's happening on the job and may, in fact, be its victim. Make office politics work for you.

·····································

While you're struggling to stay afloat in the microcosm of your workplace, the macrocosm of the entire universe of the labor market continues to group and regroup at a rapid pace. Even to stand still, you must keep up with the tides of change in the rest of the world.

··············· *Coach's Tip* ················

At least once a year find out the latest information available about the growth of the labor market, data on wage and salary workers and the facts about employment by industry.

·····································

The information you need to keep current is available in newspapers, magazines, reference books and the U.S. Department of Labor's Bureau of Labor Statistics, the mother of all employment information. Don't hesitate to call the labor department any time you need information. Your taxes pay the salaries of its employees.

Here are some data on everything you ever needed and wanted to know about the labor market, courtesy of the labor department and its research published in the *Occupational Outlook Quarterly* (Fall 1993):

- More than 50 million workers will enter the labor force during the 1992–2005 time period. They will make up about one-third of the 151 million workers who will be in the labor force in 2005.

- Employment will increase more during the 1992–2005 period than it did during the previous 13 years.

- Most workers will be employed in wage and salary jobs, which will account for most of the growth over the 1992–2005 time frame. The number of self-employed workers in the labor market will increase only to 11.7 million from 10.4 million.

- Employment will continue to shift to the service-producing sector of the economy from the goods-producing sector. Almost all new jobs will be in the service-producing sector.

- Two divisions in the service-producing sector—services and retail trade—will account for almost four-fifths of the total growth in nonagricultural wage and salary jobs.

- Employment in the goods-producing sector declined by 3 million from 1978 to 1992, but it will increase from 1992 to 2005 as the long-term decline in manufacturing jobs slows and employment rises in the construction industry.

- On average, job growth will be fastest in the major occupational groups requiring the most education and having the highest earnings.

· · · · · · · · · · · · · · · · *Coach's Tip* · · · · · · · · · · · · · · · ·

Reward yourself for working so hard to keep current by spending an entire weekend without once thinking about what's happening at the office.

· ·

Now that you are as current as you can be, both inside the office and out, it's time to turn your attention to dealing with the manager on whom your professional life depends.

7

First Shoot All the Managers

 Okay, I'm kidding. I really mean first shoot all the law-
yers. But no, I don't mean that, either. What I *do* mean
is that both managers and lawyers are highly visible
professionals—and generally higher paid than the rest of us.
That leads to a bit of resentment, if you're not either one of them!

Whether or not you're currently a manager, read this chapter.
If you're a manager, you'll pick up invaluable information. If
you're just a plain working stiff, like most of us, you'll learn a lot
about the nature of the beast called "manager." You'll also become aware of what is expected of you as your own manager.
And in the next chapter, Chapter 8, you'll learn how to win the
marvelous wrestling match I call "Dealing with the Big, Bad
Boss."

Meanwhile, back at the mat, the truth is nobody has to go so
far as shooting all the managers. Since the early 1980s, corporate
America, all by itself, has been decimating the ranks of managers and middle managers without any help from lower-level
employees. Middle managers are a dying breed, able to be replaced by a smart machine or a smarter lower-level employee in
a cyberspace moment.

For instance, take a look at Ameritech, the large, all-powerful corporation, like IBM and Sears, where aspiring managers always thought they could get a job for life.

Well, that was then, in the olden days, when Ameritech was made up of smaller, friendly units. But now is now. In addition to thousands of employees—most of them middle managers—laid off in the 1980s, between 1991 and 1994 Ameritech's payroll shrank to 67,000 from 76,000. And once again, most of those who were downsized were the incredibly shrinking, nonunion management employees.

·········· *Coach's Tip* ··········

I'm sure you get the point by now that management jobs are going to be scarce. But good managers still are needed, just as good employees are needed in manufacturing, despite the fact that manufacturing is not projected to be much of a growth industry.

You can be that good manager. Anywhere.

Let's first define what a "good" manager is. The popular cliché about managers is that they are people who are good at something else. Though the description has negative overtones, it actually is right on target. Very few people decide in the third grade that they're going to grow up to be a manager. Instead, they choose a profession, get the best start they can in it and from that vantage point hope to work up to supervisory ranks.

·········· *Coach's Tip* ··········

One way to learn to be a manager is to get hired for a management training program. This entry-level job most often is offered to new college graduates.

Unfortunately, there are fewer and fewer entry-level training programs and fewer management trainee slots in the programs that remain. So right off the bat, you have to be outstanding enough to be chosen for one of the entry-level programs—and you also have to be clear in your own mind, early on, that management is the place you want to be.

Even if you don't start out in a management training program, opportunities to become a manager are still available. Often the best way is by doing your job well, better than anyone else. Slowly you will be given management responsibilities. Then it's up to you to hone your skills.

·················· *Coach's Tip* ··················

Being able to do your job well is no guarantee that you'll be able to manage. There actually is little connection between the two.

··

"Companies have to make management a profession," says Gerard R. Egan, an internationally known management consultant. "Right now, it's a pickup game. . . . Managers must be able to develop employees and work in partnership with them instead of against them."

You can learn how to manage in increments, by taking management courses as an undergraduate and continuing to do so while employed. (See Chapter 14.)

·················· *Coach's Tip* ··················

There is no doubt that a master of business administration, that much discussed MBA, is a big-ticket item on the road to management success.

··

Earning your MBA once you've worked in the real world of hard knocks for a few years is the career sequence that makes the most sense. That way you have a much better understanding of what to major in and—even better—perhaps your employer will pay for your studies.

················ *Coach's Tip* ················

Find out early on if your company offers a special MBA program it sends employees to at a nearby graduate school of business, such as the programs that Harley-Davidson and the *Chicago Tribune* have.

··

Warning: Wait until you've been on the job for at least one year before applying for your company's MBA program. It may take several years until you are chosen, but even asking to be considered increases your visibility. This, all by itself, accelerates your upward career path and increases your value to the company.

When we talk about management in the 21st century, we're talking about radical changes. If you want to be a manager, you'll have to be flexible enough to throw away forever any ideas you have about being the much-feared, tough overseer who runs the show without any back talk from lowly employees.

Michael J. Driver, a management professor at the University of Southern California, pulls no punches when he is quoted in *Fortune* magazine about managers as decision makers: "The old industrial model primarily called for people who were very focused, structured, analytical and action-oriented," he says. But while those attributes and skills certainly aren't too shabby, there is a problem with them: They're obsolete.

Driver goes on to say that "as we move into the Information Age, we will have to develop adaptive, multifocus thinking—change is everywhere—using lots of information, seeing it going in multiple directions. An integrative style."

················ *Coach's Tip* ················

In the Information Age, you may find that you will be doing more "managing" of computer network systems to communicate your ideas and suggestions than hands-on supervision of employees.

··

You already know that you aren't going to find many managers, no matter where you are employed. And the few who do rise into executive and management levels will be those who are the computer whizzes, the managers who understand how to create, use and explain the latest information technology to the rest of the company.

···············   *Coach's Tip*   ················

Studying for your MBA may take only a few years, and then you have your degree. Staying on the cutting edge of computer technology is a lifelong must for managers.

··

High tech has also precipitated dynamic changes in the nature and status of those who report to you. Even though they do indeed depend on you for evaluations, raises and promotions, now as never before, you depend on them to do the work that may be so technical that you may not know how to do it as well as they do.

In many businesses and industries, you, as the manager, aren't going to know as much as the group or team you head. In some cases you may not even make as much money as some of them do, especially the highly skilled, highly trained technical specialists. If the idea of not knowing and not earning as much as someone you have to manage doesn't appeal to you, forget about management in the 21st century. It's not for you.

As I've stressed earlier, smart machines and emphasis on quality management have turned employees into teams of workers. As a team leader, it will be up to you to make each member of the team an actively contributing team player as well as an important individual achiever.

···············   *Coach's Tip*   ················

To succeed as a manager, you will have to create a collaborative spirit among team members.

··

Collaboration is defined in the dictionary as "to labor together." It describes the cooperation needed to be successful in a global marketplace. It replaces the former emphasis on individual competition to get ahead.

············· *Coach's Tip* ·················

One of the hardest things you'll have to learn to do is to inspire teamwork and loyalty in an atmosphere where there is no employer loyalty to the worker.
·······································

Unless your workplace is unionized, your staff will have little job security, no matter how well the employees do their jobs or how well the team performs. In fact, if they do make major achievements as a team, they actually may work themselves out of a job—and you won't be able to protect them.

Promises you make may not be enforceable, and even if you don't know that, employees do. It's one of the realities of life in today's workplace.

············· *Coach's Tip* ·················

While always being encouraging and complimentary to your staff when they deserve it, don't make promises to them that you may not be able to keep.
·······································

If you never promise anyone a rose garden, you don't have to deliver a bouquet of roses, even if you'd like to. Instead, be honest. Share what information you can about what you've picked up from hobnobbing with the higher echelons. And when something major is about to change, make sure your staff hears it first from you.

·················· *Coach's Tip* ················

To inspire trust, you must be trustworthy.
··

Most likely you will be managing not only full-time employees but another permutation of the continuing trend by employers to get rid of as many full-time employees (FTEs) as possible: *contingency workers.*

In addition to handling the details required to utilize fully the skills and abilities of people on your permanent payroll, you'll also have to obtain, schedule and supervise part-time workers, contract workers, consultants, temporary workers and even paid interns and others hired for a six-month to one-year period.

················· *Coach's Tip* ················

Staffing itself is a full-time job, and the work your department produces depends on how well you do it. Try to involve your staff and team members in all staff hiring, including contingency workers, by scheduling meetings with small groups of workers and by asking staff opinions of job candidates.
··

I've never heard of a master's degree in Contingency Workforce Management, but it's certainly one that's needed. If your company doesn't offer in-house training in how to keep your full-time workers lean and meanwhile integrating temporary workers into your everyday operations, ask to enroll in seminars or workshops on the subject or to be allowed to sign up for management courses that touch on the subject.

Once you figure out how to manage the many varieties of contingent workers you have, another part of your task is integrating their work with those of the full-timers—and getting the full-timers to accept them.

Full-time workers are well aware that contingent workers have replaced their former colleagues and may indeed replace them. You as the manager must be aware of the underlying tensions that accompany the lack of job security that now is woven into the fabric of corporate America. However, you have a head start because your staff is involved in all hiring.

·················· *Coach's Tip* ················

Treat all members of your department, regardless of their status, as clients—clients you do not want to lose. That will help you get through the tough times and will make it easier to make tough managerial decisions.

··

If you have a secretarial staff—or if you are employed as a secretary—you already know that the continued restructuring and downsizing of corporate staffs and the introduction of automation into the workplace have made significant changes in the way secretaries do their jobs. Not only are secretaries recognized as being integral parts of the team, which they always were, but they now have growing management responsibilities. According to Professional Secretaries International, today's high-tech secretary handles everything from supervision to customer relations to data management. Unfortunately, though high-tech secretaries perform many of the duties formerly held by middle managers—in addition to doing their traditional work for several bosses, instead of only one—their salaries remain low.

·················· *Coach's Tip* ················

Reward your secretary-manager with good raises and bonuses. She deserves them. Acknowledge her managerial responsibilities instead of pretending they're the usual ingredients of the job.

··

Offer secretaries professional development in computer skills, supervision, interpersonal communications and quality control. Doing so will pay off for you in their newly acquired professional skills, enthusiasm and loyalty.

·················· *Coach's Tip* ··················

Make sure all your employees have continuous training, frequent performance reviews, earned salary increases and pats on the back. They pay off for everyone, including you, the manager.

··

Women are becoming more prevalent in the ranks of managers, not just at secretarial levels but as full-fledged supervisors with employees reporting to them. In fact, women make up 44 percent of all managers in the United States, and their numbers are growing. But in 1994 only three women were chief executive officers of the nation's top 1,000 companies. That women and minorities are held back by sex discrimination from advancing into higher-echelon management jobs is called the *glass ceiling.*

Refusing to promote employees because of their gender, race, national origin, religion, ethnic background, age, disabilities or sexual orientation is illegal. In addition to the legal repercussions, by refusing to consider all qualified candidates in your diversified workplace, you are denying yourself and your company the contributions of vital, talented and competent employees. That's called *bad management.*

Because women are so rare and so new in top-level jobs, they are watched a lot more closely. There is much talk about what it's like to work for a woman manager in terms of gender, rather than in terms of performance, as is done with the majority of managers—men.

Studies show that a majority of workers want to work for a woman because she is more inclusive, more of a team player, more considerate and more encouraging about career advancement. Other studies, equally impressive, show that people do not want to work for women because they usually do not have the power male bosses have or access to important information. Still, other studies show that people who work for women managers complain that the women are just like the men in being cold and uncaring; otherwise, they would never have been given management positions.

·················· *Coach's Tip* ·················

As you can see, managing can be a lose-lose job. That's why it's so important to observe the golden rule of management: Be fair!

·····································

Regardless of the manager's gender, the fact that projected changes in the composition of the labor force by 2000 indicate that white men will make up only 15 percent of all new hires will require you to have a more humanistic approach to management of employees.

Leo Burnett, founder and chair of Leo Burnett Co., an international advertising company, got it right in 1956 when he said, "We recognize that everybody here is looking for human dignity, a feeling of belonging, an open-minded attitude, an atmosphere of human and friendly relationships, a sense of participating and a feeling of 'worthwhileness' about his or her efforts."

·················· *Coach's Tip* ·················

Management has to set the tone that diversity is valued and that you constantly must have an eye out for talented minority and female candidates.

·····································

Looking at women and minorities as individuals involves being sensitive to what makes them unique. The United States long has been romantically described as the melting pot of the world. That may have been true in the past of white ethnic groups, but it certainly isn't completely true today and will be less true in the 21st century.

Most racial, ethnic and national groups want to retain the qualities that make them unique. They also want to be part of the mainstream and eventually will be, if they already are not. But most have no desire to forget where they come from and what they bring with them.

··

The cartoon character Popeye always runs around saying matter of factly, "I yam what I yam." We each are, and smart managers will act with that important information in mind. Total assimilation no longer is the goal of most segments of the diverse U.S. workforce. Making a good living is.

Acknowledging diversity is a must for today's manager, especially an upwardly mobile one. If you are a white male— and the majority of managers and CEOs are—how do you know what people want who do not look exactly like you, do not have the exact priorities and, even worse, probably don't belong to your golf club? In fact, some, called "women," can't even get into the men's room, where so much important business information is exchanged.

Unlike Sigmund Freud, who always wanted to know what women in particular wanted but never asked them, ask women and minorities on your staff what they want. Talk to them. Get to know them as the individuals they are.

··

I myself got so tired of talking and writing about diversity in a vacuum that I decided to ask representatives of various groups what makes them different from white men in their needs and desires in the workplace and how these differences might impact on performance.

·················   *Coach's Tip*   ················

Performance, after all, is the bottom line for managers of a diversified workforce.

···

Here's what I learned:

- *Women don't want to be treated as if they are male clones.* They are eager to work as members of teams, to share power, to share ideas. They will get the job done, but they will do it their own way, and most will try to avoid trampling on others as they do it. Most importantly, they perform best in an atmosphere where family responsibilities are acknowledged and the company supports them with work and family options and benefits.

- *Asian Americans are a diverse group within themselves.* They are not all mathematical geniuses and superacheivers. Some are highly educated, as we know, but others are illiterate, even in their own language. Since most are not holders of advanced degrees in physics or brain surgery—like most other Americans—training programs are essential and are welcome in entry-level jobs. Asian Americans also hit the glass ceiling, though they're eagerly recruited for their technical skills and abilities. Affirmative action is needed to allow them to move up the corporate ladder.

- *Hispanics have a language and frequently a religion in common, but they also are a diverse group.* In the United States most have been discriminated against because they are graduates of inner-city schools and often are unprepared to meet job requirements. Hispanics also need job training and affirmative action. They describe themselves as loyal employees, hardworking and family oriented. Even highly educated and highly recruited Hispanics—and there are thousands of them—say that they find it hard to promote their abilities and accomplishments in the workplace, ask for a raise or complain about unfair practices. They'd leave before doing so.

• *African Americans were brought to the United States as slaves and have been treated as second-class citizens ever since.* Often blamed for not being able to pull themselves up by their bootstraps even when they have no boots, many African Americans have fought their way past discriminatory employers—with the important assistance of antidiscrimination laws—and have become valuable contributors to U.S. business and industry. The emphasis on getting a good education, despite poor inner-city schools in segregated communities, has given many African Americans a ticket out of poverty.

There's a myth that if a woman or minority is hired or promoted, it's only to meet affirmative action requirements and that the person isn't qualified. The truth is that the person *is* qualified, and you will get credit for being a good manager because you are smart enough to recognize and hire talent.

And now that you know how to manage everyone equally, let's find out how to deal with the big, bad bosses so many employees have.

8

Dealing with the Big, Bad Boss

 No matter how wonderful you are or how many talents you possess that you do not want to hide, if you have a nightmare of a boss, you're not going to get anywhere. In fact, all you will get is frustrated—unless you know how to deal with the tyrant who is your supervisor.

My phone rings off the hook with complaints from people who say their bosses are driving them crazy. One woman told me she complained so often about the deprecating remarks her boss continually made to her face and behind her back that her husband said if she told him one more horror story he would personally come in the office and punch him out. As a result, the woman stopped complaining about him at home but continued to suffer at work.

There's no need to suffer in silence, either at home or in the workplace. I personally don't believe in doing either; I much prefer making loud and frequent complaints. But as a true professional, you can learn to manage—and survive—the wolf in wolf's clothing: The Big, Bad Boss (TBBB).

These are some of the terrorist tactics of TBBB:

- denigrating you in front of your colleagues

- denigrating you behind closed doors

- refusing to give you good assignments

- ignoring your input and productivity

- making fun of you outside the office

- telling you flat out that he or she can't stand you—and saying so without a smile

················· *Coach's Tip* ················

An important thing to know about destructive managers who daily chip away at your confidence and crush your ego is that you probably aren't the only object of their scorn and abuse.

But if they've been allowed to run rampant for years, it's probably because no one higher up in the company considers the situation important enough to do anything to change it. Or it's because no one has had the nerve to complain forcefully enough about TBBB to get some kind of action. Instead, about the worst thing that happens to really bad executives who wreak havoc is that they often are moved from department to department—where they wreak more havoc in more parts of the organization.

·············· *Coach's Tip* ···············

If it's any comfort to you, these seemingly protected species of managers eventually do themselves in because their unhappy staffs become less productive, and that catches the eyes of the top brass as nothing else does.

··

However, that may take a few years, and by that time you may be in no condition to benefit from TBBB's absence. That's why I'm going to give you a few pointers on how to extricate yourself from this difficult situation. And I'll start with the most radical suggestion of all: Make complaints to TBBB's supervisors.

·············· *Coach's Tip* ···············

The last thing most people would ever consider doing is making a complaint about the boss—unless you are protected by a union and can follow a formal grievance procedure. But 84 percent of all U.S. workers are not unionized. That means you have to represent yourself.

··

Begin by talking informally, and preferably not in the office, with other people who are public victims of TBBB. Have lunch with a handful of colleagues you absolutely trust, and do what you always do: Complain about the boss. Talk about the trap of being in a situation where the person who feels it necessary to deprecate you also is the one who controls your raises and career advancement.

But this time, instead of only complaining, which you are perfectly justified in doing, try to come up with some suggestions on how to handle TBBB.

·············· *Coach's Tip* ················

TBBB is not going to change very much but for self-preservation might heed a strong warning from company executives. Your hope is that management will impress on TBBB that abusive behavior is not acceptable or, even better, will transfer the monster—or, just as good, transfer you to a comparable job with a bearable boss.

··

If your firm has a human resources department, make an appointment to talk about the situation. But don't go alone. In this delicate matter, there is safety in numbers. A minimum number for protection is three.

·············· *Coach's Tip* ················

When you talk to the human resources people about TBBB, be cool.

··

Discuss the situation dispassionately. Cite specific dates and instances of unfair and humiliating practices. Don't show anger or be confrontational. Don't whine. Simply state the facts, explaining how the lowered morale affects the staff's productivity. It will be understood that if you and your colleagues are risking your jobs to report your own boss, the situation must be serious. You will be heard.

The only reason I advise such desperate measures as talking to a personnel representative is that my assessment of these situations is that you have nothing to lose. Under an abusive boss, your career, at best, is at a standstill, and so is your paycheck. And the effects of being mistreated on your mental health are cumulative and also extremely harmful.

If you don't have a human resources department, your only choice then is to go directly to the person to whom TBBB reports. Once again, this is a tricky situation; but once again, you probably have nothing to lose. Follow the above advice. Don't go alone. Be prepared and remain calm. You also may want to talk to the executive TBBB reports to even if you've already spoken to the human resources department. Once again, you have nothing to lose.

Either directly or indirectly—and let's hope it's directly—word will get back to TBBB that the staff is restless and things will have to change. And things will change, because now TBBB, who basically is a bully, knows someone is watching.

If knowing you've complained leads TBBB to punish you with verbal abuse or bad assignments, how can you tell? That's what TBBB already is doing and why you complained about him or her in the first place.

Companies are afraid of discrimination lawsuits and are also eager to quench any sign of rebellion among the troops. When they hear enough complaints about TBBB, they finally may feel compelled to take action. And later they can't say they didn't know what was going on. You may not get action right away. Meanwhile, you may even be in the company doghouse because so many people confuse the messenger with the message. But I have seen that for those who are brave enough to tough it out, going to those in power eventually works.

· · · · · · · · · · · · · · · · *Coach's Tip* · · · · · · · · · · · · · · · · ·

Be realistic about what you're doing.
· ·

At the same time that you're trying to nullify the toxic effects of TBBB, you also should be making inquiries about job openings in other departments or divisions of the company. And it wouldn't hurt to update your resume. Remember, you would be taking these steps even if you hadn't taken any action against TBBB.

One nightmare of having an obnoxious boss is that it's so difficult to fight back, directly or indirectly. But no matter how hard it is to do so, you have to learn to handle the situation, even if you don't always win.

"I lined up some allies, we complained to the proper authorities, but nothing happened," a paralegal told me. "Our manager is particularly vicious, and the lawyers he reports to seemingly like it that way." Despite the complaints of the firm's entire support staff of seven, this paralegal said that nothing was ever done about TBBB.

"I guess we were lucky we weren't fired, but most of us couldn't take it anymore," she said. "I found another job, a much better one. While I hate [the fact] that TBBB—that creep—still is in power and torturing everyone he can, I learned a lot from the process of speaking up. I don't think anyone will ever be able to push me around again."

Fight back wisely. And if it doesn't work indirectly by going to TBBB's superiors, you will have to handle the situation yourself. In person. But no matter how much I encourage you not to take the machinations of TBBB lying down, you still may not want to go one-on-one in defending yourself. So if top executives won't step in, try to mitigate the effect of TBBB's need to dominate you by subtle and brilliant countermoves.

Andra Medea is a conflict management consultant who works both with companies and individual workers. Medea, who holds both bachelor and masters degrees in conflict management, used to teach self-defense against street violence and physical assault. She sees a clear connection between street fighting and office "violence." They're both about power, she says. "It's the same in business as in the streets."

················· *Coach's Tip* ·················

Nonviolence works in the streets, as Dr. Martin Luther King proved in the United States. And it also works in the office, as Medea's suggestions prove.

··

According to Medea, on a one-to-one basis, don't let TBBB see that she or he is successful in upsetting you. That merely encourages her or him to continue. Look the other way when TBBB pounds the table or screams and yells at you. Pretend it never happened. That also helps stop the behavior because without a victim, destructive behavior isn't as much fun.

················· *Coach's Tip* ················

It's okay and perfectly normal to get deeply angry at being mistreated by TBBB. But it's folly to show it. You'll make TBBB too happy by doing so.
··

One of the best things you achieve by not visibly reacting is that it throws TBBB off guard. He's used to watching his victims squirm, a form of sadism that assures him that he is the boss. While all this is happening, you can be charitable in your thoughts and think to yourself that TBBB may simply be a very nice person who has no idea how to manage.

You could also try a bit of humor, though TBBB is not known for a sense of humor. However, it may make you feel better.

A much-abused faculty assistant told me that the professor who heads his department enjoyed making fun of the way he dressed for work—in addition to constantly berating him for anything else he could think of. "I had gotten used to his other insults because he treated everyone the same way, but I was the only one whose clothes he criticized, even though I dressed like him and everyone else," the assistant said. "But my approach was never to say anything back because I figured it would only make things worse."

But much of the nasty treatment ended when the assistant decided to joke about the denigrating remarks the professor made instead of letting them pass as usual. "In our last really vicious encounter, after my boss accused me of being late for class, not meeting with students, not doing my job and wearing hideous ties, I burst out laughing because it was so ludicrous for me, as an adult, to be going through such humiliation," the assistant said.

As he laughed, he reached for a pair of scissors on the professor's desk. The assistant slowly brought the scissors up to his much-maligned tie and methodically cut it into little pieces. "There," he told TBBB. "Now you know there's nothing I won't do to please you!"

TBBB stared for a few seconds in disbelief and then burst out laughing. From what the faculty assistant tells me, the professor still is laughing, their relationship has become a far more pleasant one and the ripple effect is that TBBB is less abusive to other faculty members, too. In fact, TBBB really doesn't fit into that category anymore.

· · · · · · · · · · · · · · · · · *Coach's Tip* · · · · · · · · · · · · · · · · ·

Take a risk and do something unexpected. Once again, you have nothing to lose.

· ·

One of my favorite stories of astounding TBBB comes from Medea's consulting experience. A client of hers had a boss who had a fit right in her face. He screamed and yelled at her, his faced turned red and his veins bulged. "In the midst of his tirade, she reached over, took his wrist and started to take his pulse," Medea relates. "She even looked seriously concerned."

The switch in the power relationship ended his tirade and ultimately his daily attacks on her performance and character. Basically a coward at heart, TBBB knew she was someone he should not mess around with. So he stopped.

· · · · · · · · · · · · · · · · · *Coach's Tip* · · · · · · · · · · · · · · · · ·

Most bad bosses are blind to their uncaring behavior. It's up to you to take off their blindfolds as painlessly as possible—that is, for you.

· ·

TBBB is an extreme example of how harmful your supervisor can be to the health of your career. Most situations aren't so relentlessly offensive, but they still are cause for concern. If your boss is doing something that really upsets you or has a negative effect on your performance, you can't ignore it. You have to do something about it.

"It may not sound important, but it was extremely annoying to me each time my boss joked about how many kids I had—which she never missed an opportunity to do," said a retail salesclerk. "I let it go a couple of times because I didn't want to appear thin-skinned. But it was a put-down, and I was offended every time she kidded me publicly about my wife and me having the huge amount of four kids under ten years of age. I took it in silence for a long time because otherwise she was such a good boss."

The salesclerk said he brooded about the seemingly harmless joking for several weeks, and after discussing it with his wife, he decided to voice his concern about being made fun of—for any reason. He asked to meet with his boss and in a calm manner told her that he and his wife had completed their family and didn't intend to have more children. He then told her straight-out that although she probably wasn't aware of it, she made him very uncomfortable every time she joked about the size of his family.

He didn't ask her to stop. He didn't have to. His boss immediately apologized and never teased him again, about anything. "I think she wasn't aware that any kind of put-down from a boss really hurts," the clerk said. "I've noticed since then that she's much more careful about what she says to everyone. It worked out well."

· · · · · · · · · · · · · · · *Coach's Tip* · · · · · · · · · · · · · · · · ·

When your boss offends, don't let your resentment build up. Nip it in the bud by politely telling your boss as soon as it's strategically possible how it affects you. Assuming you are dealing with someone who is not TBBB, in most cases that will be the end of it.

· ·

Handling each situation as it arises is a smart way to maintain a healthy, working relationship with your boss. The secret to taming bosses is never to barge into their offices shaking with anger. Calm down first, and discuss the situation as an equal.

Though I'll coach you on how to make performance reviews work for you more thoroughly in Chapter 10, I want to stress here that the performance review is a very good time to bring up any concerns you have about the way your boss treats you. Make sure you can cite specific incidents and explain how they affected you.

·················· *Coach's Tip* ··················

A dialogue is what you want with your boss, not a confrontation—from either side.

··

Worried employees frequently tell me that they're completely in the dark about how their bosses *really* feel about them. I tell them that if they have performance reviews, it really doesn't matter what the boss feels. What matters is what they put in writing.

Not every company has performance reviews—though the smart ones do—but every company does keep personnel records.

Many states mandate that personnel records be made available when employees request to see them. If your state has that law, at least once a year make a formal request to see what's in your file. You may be surprised.

"I found a memo from my boss that I had messed up on deadlines on a very important project—but I hadn't even worked on it," a research assistant said. "I couldn't remove the note because you're not allowed to touch the file except to copy documents. But I was able to put in a note of my own explaining the truth of the situation." He also discussed it with his boss, who apologized profoundly and corrected the memo.

"When I looked at my file, I was in shock," an administrative assistant said. "Three of my four supervisors had the same complaint about me—that I talked too much on the phone. Not one of them had said a word to me directly about it." She says it was probably true that she spent too much time on the phone, though perhaps some of her friendly conversations with clients were interpreted as being personal calls. But instead of arguing about it, she "cleaned up" her act and now keeps all phone conversations short—including the business ones. Her change was quickly noted by her supervisor, who congratulated her for "saving time."

·················· *Coach's Tip* ················

You don't have a leg to stand on when you complain about or are offended by criticisms that are true.

··

Assuming you are your own best friend, someone in the office may be your own worst enemy—the *office stool pigeon*, the one who feeds the boss misinformation about you. It's hard to counteract false information that one professional friend gives another, but if your boss is one half of that duo and you are the target, you have to defend yourself.

················· *Coach's Tip* ················

The person you see as a stool pigeon or toady and who obviously does not like you may actually be an intimate of your boss who simply wants to be helpful. Regardless of motivation, the end result is the same, and your only option is to try to diffuse the negative messages your boss is receiving.

··

It's a no-win situation to try to break up a friendship between your boss and the informant, to try to get the stool pigeon to ease off or to plant seeds of doubt with your boss about the authenticity of criticism about you. It's also hard to get your boss to believe that what you say is true, rather than what the trusted colleague says—all at the same time.

· · · · · · · · · · · · · · · *Coach's Tip* · · · · · · · · · · · · · · ·

Though it would be wonderful to stop the vendetta against you by confronting your enemy—perhaps early in the morning at 50 paces, though I prefer nonviolence—it's far wiser to ignore the stool pigeon. Instead, once again your best route is to focus on getting the correct information directly to the boss.

· ·

As delightful as it would be, you can't run into the boss's office and say, "Someone told me Joe Blow told you I was fudging on my expense accounts, but he's a liar. My expense accounts are absolutely accurate."

A more subtle method, but one with much more chance of success, is to hand your next expense account report directly to your boss instead of to an intermediate. Point out the various items listed, and explain every single one. Stress how you always are concerned about saving the company money. Be informal but not casual.

Your point is made. Now the boss knows you are very careful before spending even a single penny of your employer's money and that you accurately and ethically report each expenditure.

· · · · · · · · · · · · · · · *Coach's Tip* · · · · · · · · · · · · · · ·

If enough people in the office show up at the boss's desk to explain various details of how they do their job, the boss eventually may take the stool pigeon's reports less seriously—and not just about expense accounts.

· ·

As much as we may joke about the Big, Bad Boss or even the Big, Occasionally Bad Boss, it's unsettling to see the office as a constant battlefield. You know firsthand that it isn't, that often things go very well and for weeks in a row you may have very few complaints.

But even the many good times must not lull you into assuming that all is always well and that you are always perfectly understood. (Some people tell me their problem is that they *are* understood!) I'm not suggesting you be on guard every moment for unprovoked attacks from your supervisors or their informants. I'm simply urging you to be aware that you can and must deal with any unwarranted attacks on your performance or character that arise. They won't go away by themselves.

•••••••••••••••• *Coach's Tip* ••••••••••••••••

Even in the best of all times, keep records of the work you've completed, your special projects, details of discussions with your boss and any other pertinent information. It may come in handy—and if it doesn't, so much the better.

••

Now that you know how to deal with your boss, even the worst one imaginable, it's time to organize your job so that you can be successful in your climb upward.

• • • • • *9* • • • • •

Organizing Your Job
To Succeed

You're finally in a job that's right for you and that you love. You know all you can possibly know about the financial stability of the company and its future plans. And as icing on the cake, you get along with your boss. What more can you ask for? A lot!

The working paradise—well, maybe it's not a paradise, but it's certainly not hell—you've created can disappear in a moment without the proper care and attention it needs. And that nurturing must come from you. Now is the time to get down to the business of setting yourself up for success rather than failure. And the way to do this is to be proactive rather than passive and reactive.

• • • • • • • • • • • • • • • • • *Coach's Tip* • • • • • • • • • • • • • • • •

The first step in organizing for success is to take hold of the day-to-day details of your job.

• •

Everyone makes fun of list makers, including me, at times. Years ago I wrote a poem entitled "List-less" that was published in a national magazine. It read as follows:

List-less
I keep a list of things to do
And carefully accrue them.
I keep the list so carefully
I don't have time to do them!

Profit from my mistakes. Keep lists of things to do and actually do them, every day. If you don't organize your job, which means writing down on a daily basis every detail you must attend to in order to get the work done by the end of the week, you have no chance of handling the mountain of work expected from you.

•••••••••••••• *Coach's Tip* ••••••••••••••••

Don't lose your list.
•••

To avoid setting yourself up for failure, make your schedule of daily duties reasonable. Leave time for unexpected meetings or important lunch dates. As in everything else in the office, be flexible. Nonetheless, by the end of the work week, get the work done that you know must be done.

Keeping a list and crossing off each item when completed in itself gives you a sense of accomplishment that you need when you have a lot of work to do.

•••••••••••••• *Coach's Tip* ••••••••••••••••

Because the goal is to be up-to-date and efficient, you may have to come in early, skip some lunches, stay late or even do some work now and then on your days off.
•••

As you may have guessed by now, I am completely on the side of you, the employee. I don't want workers exploited by managers who cut their staffs to the bare minimum and expect the survivors to pick up the slack. But as I see it, workers today have no choice. Only those who work long hours now and then and are flexible enough to assume responsibility for new tasks will succeed.

I wish it were different, but it isn't. And it's not going to change for many decades, I fear. Robert B. Reich, secretary of labor, in explaining his decision to delay resolving some really tough management-labor issues, made some comments that you always should keep in mind when organizing your job to succeed. "Worker-management relations today are very tense, given all the corporate downsizings, the increased litigation in the workplace, the technological changes and the enormous pressures on companies to cut costs," he told Louis Uchitelle of the *New York Times.*

While making your list of things to do on a daily basis, you'll very quickly pick up the work that needs to be done that no one is doing—and that, to the detriment of your department's productivity, is being lost in the shuffle. If you let function determine form, as artists advise us to do, you quickly will be aware of what actually is needed to get the job done. And your awareness of those details, followed by offering to do them and doing them well, will guarantee your success.

•••••••••••••••• *Coach's Tip* ••••••••••••••••

Organized people—those who know exactly what is expected of them in their job and what they need from their colleagues or team to achieve it—are among the most valued of all valuable employees.

•••

Ten years ago, when his company was investigating becoming fully automated, an assistant in the human resources department was asked to handle a few details of the new project. He had plenty of work to do already and technical office equipment wasn't his specialty, but he accepted the new assignment with enthusiasm and learned all he could about hardware and software and about mainframes versus personal computers.

The assistant helped the company select computers and programs. He next helped choose the ergonomically correct office furniture for the staff. He helped design computer-age work stations. He supervised computer training of the staff, including the top executives, whom he impressed because they depended on him for his knowledge in a field they knew nothing about.

Today this assistant no longer recruits or hires new personnel. His job has expanded to include other aspects of keeping an office going. His new title is facility manager, and he's responsible for everything in the building—from computers to furniture to office space to the outside real estate holdings of the firm.

In the same way, a former secretary told me she had understood so clearly what her job was and what additional work had to be done that, after several years of coordinating her large corporation's meetings, receptions, conventions and workshops, she added all the details of what had to be done and came up with a new job for herself. She's now the firm's meeting planner, is ranked as a manager and has a staff of her own and a good salary. She also efficiently gets done a great deal of important work that no one previously was well organized enough to pay attention to or see the glaring need for.

· · · · · · · · · · · · · · · · · *Coach's Tip* · · · · · · · · · · · · · · · · ·

Being organized and efficient not only helps make your job secure, it's also your ticket to moving upward in the organization.

· ·

Individual efforts have long been part of the American Dream, but today that dream has a few sequels. One is that teamwork—while not completely replacing individual contributions, for which a worker is still judged—is increasing in popularity among proponents of quality management and has to be taken into consideration in the way you organize your work.

················ *Coach's Tip* ················

Be up-to-date on every assignment, goal and deadline your team has so that you know how to schedule your own tasks.
··

One good thing about teams is that you have team meetings. Listen carefully to what assignments are given to each member. Pay attention to what your teammates have to say about how a job should be done. Be aware of what they see as their roadblocks or problems. Share your concerns and expertise with them, too. Above all, pay attention to what the team leader suggests has to be done and in what order. Offer to help your colleagues and ask them to help you.

················ *Coach's Tip* ················

If you're part of a team, be a good team player. Besides, you have no choice about it.
··

Your individual and team efforts to do the job well are powerful forces in gaining the muscle power needed to move ahead. And there are other "helpmates," too. One of the best leverages you can have in conditioning yourself for success is to have a *mentor,* someone already in the company who knows the ropes and is willing to help you learn them. If the mentor also is someone who ranks above you or is in management in another department of the company, so much the better.

A wise saying advises that if you don't have a mentor, hire one. It's not bad advice. Of course, you can't pay someone to be your mentor, but you need one so much that it would be well worth your while to lay out a few bucks to acquire one. Unfortunately, no one has been smart enough to start a rent-a-mentor business, though I'm certain it would be an overnight success.

If no one offers to be your mentor and those you ask to be your mentor are not interested in such a full-time responsibility, create your own mentor. Creating your own mentor does not involve secretive laboratory procedures, such as those that created Frankenstein. Besides, you don't want a Frankenstein; you want a helpful, receptive mentor.

One way to solve the problem of not having a single individual to help guide you is to put together a composite mentor from those who don't mind advising you in a particular aspect of the marathon game called Success.

•••••••••••••••• *Coach's Tip* ••••••••••••••••

It's better to have several mentors or advisers than none at all.

••

A registered nurse at a large city hospital had lots of friends on staff but no one who would take her under wing. After floundering around for the first few months, the nurse decided to do something about her mentorless state.

- A supervising nurse in her department, a veteran of ten years there, agreed to teach her the ropes of the daily job and suggest what she needed to learn to do her job better.

- A bookkeeper in the administrative offices promised to answer her questions about health-care costs and how they affect patient treatment.

- A medical doctor she knew in another division of the hospital agreed to inform her of changes and advances in medical practice. He agreed to let her know the future plans of the hospital and how they might impact on the nursing staff in general and on her job in particular.

It took three people, but the registered nurse is being mentored. And she says that it has made all the difference in her successful organization of her job.

••••••••••••••••• *Coach's Tip* ••••••••••••••••

If you can't find a mentor, even a composite one within your department or company, look elsewhere.

•••

You may be able to find a mentor at a professional association or network you belong to. Perhaps a qualified friend can fill the bill. Though it would be ideal, your mentor doesn't have to be in your field, but a mentor does have to be very savvy about the inner workings of the business or industrial world. And if all else fails, what about an electronic mentor?

According to Joan E. Rigdon, writing in *The Wall Street Journal*, you're not all alone if there's a mentor just a keyboard away. "A potential mentor may be as close as that personal computer on your desk," she reports. Rigdon's referring here to online bulletin boards or in-house electronic mail.

••••••••••••••••• *Coach's Tip* ••••••••••••••••

When using online networks or E-mail to ask questions or get advice about your job, be cautious.

•••

You never know who's reading them or who may be offended by your "public" statements about private business matters. And, of course, you also don't know how valid the advice may be. Since these mentors are unknown, you have no inkling as to what their credentials or underlying motives really are.

••••••••••••••••• *Coach's Tip* ••••••••••••••••

When you get good advice, use it. But don't be surprised when you outgrow the need for your mentor. It's something to celebrate!

•••

Another way to set yourself up for the race for the gold—success in your job—is to form alliances among your colleagues, especially those in your department. Men do this fairly easily: it's called the old boys' network.

Men exchange information casually and often, as they have done from the days they played team sports. They do so in the office whenever they see one another. Since most bosses are men and bosses have the most information to share, I always say if only I could get into the men's room, I'd probably be the publisher of one of the largest newspapers in the United States by now. But so far I have not been invited into the men's room, where so many future plans are discussed and other helpful information exchanged.

Men also exchange inside tips and even have been known to hire or to give large accounts to friends right there on the golf course. Women and minorities are left out of the process because of discriminatory practices in membership rules of powerful and private golf courses. For women in particular, gender discrimination in playing times for golf makes sure women and men literally do not get a chance to talk about business on an equal playing field.

Golf has become such a vital tool for finding out what you need to know to organize your job that it's no wonder they call the golf course, where all that vital information is exchanged, the "greens."

•••••••••••••••• *Coach's Tip* ••••••••••••••••

Learn to play golf, if you can. Learn to play tennis, too. And then learn how to bond with your co-workers.

••

Bonding with co-workers is another way to describe in-house networks. These have been especially popular among women employees in the same company, women who work in offices where they watch some men with merely mediocre talents get promotion after promotion.

"I was so tired of training the men under me to qualify for jobs over me that I took a group of women to lunch and said we had to do something about our lack of progress," an assistant manager told me. "It took guts to ask our employers' permission to meet on company time in a company meeting room, but the fact that we wanted everyone to know up front that we wanted to get together to talk about our careers—and that there were so many of us—got their attention and their approval. And it's worked out well. Many of us have moved ahead because we know in advance what the openings will be, unlike in the past when we heard about them only after a man got the promotion."

·············· *Coach's Tip* ··············

If you organize an in-house network, invite as your guest speaker for your very first meeting the highest-ranking official in the company.

Corporate honchos will attend your meeting because they can't say no to meeting with a group of employees—though they might think nothing of brushing you off when you try to set up an individual appointment with them.

·············· *Coach's Tip* ··············

There's power in numbers. And when the honcho shows up at your meeting, don't be shy about asking important questions.

The assistant manager who set up the in-house network at her office told me her first question of the CEO who spoke to the group was, "Who is my supervisor? I report to three different people, and no one has ever told me who actually is in charge." She says that the CEO was shocked, and ten minutes after the meeting ended, she knew who her supervisor was. "Even better," she announced, "I now have that supervisor's job—which I deserved two years ago."

Now you know about the various positive things you can do, the setting up of exercises for success rather than failure. But serious obstacles may be in your way, and you will have to handle them.

·················· *Coach's Tip* ················

Being aware of what obstacles may arise is the first giant step in diffusing them.

···

One of the most pernicious roadblocks is discrimination. My theory is that if you feel you're being treated with prejudice on the job, you probably are. There are local, state and federal laws that forbid employment discrimination, just as they do in hiring. But that, of course, doesn't always stop it.

You want a job, not a lawsuit, but discrimination and sexual harassment are intolerable. They will keep you from advancing—which is their basic purpose. You have to do something to protect yourself because either you will constantly be passed over for promotions or salary increases, or you'll either quit or be fired. Here is what you can do:

- *Keep a record of discriminatory practices, including sexual harassment, as they happen.* That means write them down, including the dates.

- *If you feel you can, confront the perpetrator and ask for the remarks to end immediately.* That might be the end of the problem.

- *But if nothing changes, next write a letter to the offender detailing what he or she has done and asking that the behavior stop immediately.* Cite witnesses, if there are any. Send a copy to your supervisor, and keep one for yourself.

- *If no action is taken, now is the time to go to the human resources department—especially if the offender is your supervisor.* Tell personnel exactly what you want: You want the discriminatory remarks and practices to stop. You want the sexual harassment to stop, and you want the offender reprimanded.

················· *Coach's Tip* ·················

As satisfying as it would be to do so, don't ask for the alleged offender to be fired. Both sides need to be heard. And now that your managers know what's going on and that you are serious about doing something about it, they might come to the conclusion on their own that the last thing they need is a discrimination lawsuit.
···

If the unwelcome behavior continues and you feel management isn't going to take any steps to end it—a very foolish decision on their part, considering the huge amounts of money for damages that victims of discriminations are being awarded—call your local federal Equal Employment Office (EEOC) and find out how to proceed.

················· *Coach's Tip* ·················

If you can afford a lawyer to represent you, get one at this point.
···

You will need an attorney to protect you from being fired for trying to stop the discrimination. And if the EEOC says that you do have a case, you will need the lawyer to handle the ensuing litigation.

················· *Coach's Tip* ·················

The very best reason for hiring a lawyer immediately is that frequently she or he can settle the case out of court, which is what most companies prefer doing.
···

Discrimination and in particular sexual harassment are obstacles in your way that, in my mind, come from hate. But you may encounter other problems in trying to be on top of your job, and they may come from love. Love is wonderful, every time around, but when sex rears its sexy head at work, you may find it can be a real barrier to your success.

The problem with office romances is that they're not usually between two people at the same level. When they're between two equals, most people are very happy that two nice, hopefully single people have found each other, either temporarily or permanently.

But when one's a manager and the other is not, a rumble of discontent arises among co-workers: One of their peers has access to much more information than they do. One of their peers is being treated with favoritism. These reactions lead to bitterness and poor morale.

"How can I possibly ever move ahead when my co-worker sleeps with the boss?" a secretary asked me. Figuring that she couldn't win that battle, she quit her job and found a better one—and the company lost a valued employee.

· · · · · · · · · · · · · · · · *Coach's Tip* · · · · · · · · · · · · · · · ·

Don't believe for one moment that you can keep an office romance secret. It can't be done. Your colleagues probably will know about it before you do!

· ·

Though you may be bursting with excitement about your new love affair, it will not end well. When management finds out, one of you will be transferred or even pressured to quit. The one who bears the brunt of the relationship usually is the one with the least status. That's usually the woman involved.

And another unhappy ending: Even if management hasn't interfered in your office romance, what do you do when it ends? You both have to deal with each other every day while nursing your wounds. Colleagues may take sides, which causes even more disruption. Office romances usually add up to a lose-lose situation.

················· *Coach's Tip* ···············

Try to avoid getting romantically or sexually involved with anyone you work with. If you're a woman, try *very* hard to avoid an office romance.

··

Just as office romances often backfire, so does hiring relatives. This is called *nepotism,* and many states and federal district courts have ruled that to discriminate in the hiring or promoting of someone because they are married to an employee is illegal. It is, in fact, a form of sex discrimination, because in most cases the person being denied a job is a woman.

Since there are so many dual-career couples in the United States, antinepotism rules can be a form of sex discrimination. Each case has to be reviewed individually for its legality. Nonetheless, if you are a relative of a current employee or work with someone who is, that extra leverage, that inside line to inside information, is disruptive.

You now know how to organize your job to succeed. You know the pitfalls that are entailed. Your coach has carefully delineated the many things you can do to make sure that you have an equal shot at handling your job in the most professional manner.

Now that you have the day-to-day details of your work under control, let's talk about the future and how to let people know what makes you special and where you want to go.

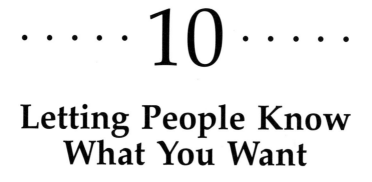

10

Letting People Know What You Want

I hate to mention this again, but as your coach I must remind you that job security doesn't exist. But that doesn't mean you should reduce your efforts to succeed in your job in any way—especially if you want to make sure that you are the one in line for the raises and promotions that are available.

••••••••••••••••• *Coach's Tip* •••••••••••••••••

Just as you marketed yourself to get the right job, now you will have to continue to market yourself to keep it.

••

"I can speak up for everyone in the department—and I often do go to bat for colleagues when they're too afraid to open their mouths," an assistant hotel manager told me. "But when it comes to me and to what I want, I have a really hard time saying anything." He went on to add that he has missed out on chances to get promoted and to be transferred to other states where the chain has hotels.

···············   *Coach's Tip*   ···············

Nobody can give you what you want unless they know what it is.

···

Getting the word out about how much you'd like to help open that new hotel in Kauai, manage the bar at the hotel in Switzerland or be the next sales manager in your department is something you will have to ask for, perhaps many times. No one will give it to you unless you make it clear that that's the direction you're headed and that's the job you want.

···············   *Coach's Tip*   ···············

Asking for what you want or finding out what it takes to get where you want to go is not the same as boasting, tooting your own horn or being overly aggressive. The latter three are counterproductive because they alienate the very people who can help you, but asking is the best way to communicate what you want.

···

Since it's a given that there's no such thing as job security, no matter how well you do your job or how much you are told what an important cog you are in the machinery that makes the company go 'round, even speaking up for yourself won't change that labor market reality—but you will be recognized as a player.

"In the overheated office environment of the nineties, people are most concerned about how they can stay out of trouble and on the payroll—and they should be," writes veteran career consultant Marilyn Moats Kennedy in her newsletter, *Kennedy's Career Strategist* (For a free sample issue, write or call 1150 Wilmette Avenue, Wilmette, IL 60091; 708-251-1661).

Not stirring up trouble or having out and out confrontations with your boss are absolutely necessary to stay on the payroll. However, that is a totally different matter from applying for job openings you're interested in, trying to find out what projects are being planned so that you can ask to be a part of them and not being afraid to say you think you are qualified to do a different job or to move ahead—or both.

·················· *Coach's Tip* ················

I cannot dispel any fears you may have of losing your job at any time. That is the nature of today's employment beast. But I urge you to conquer any fears you may have of expressing in a positive way your interest in doing the work you really want to do—and that needs to be done. After all, you are on the inside, and you know what's going on.

··

As your player-coach, I, too, used to wrestle with how and when to speak up for something I really wanted, thought I deserved to get and never got. As your player-coach, I, too, found it much easier and even more important to go to bat for my colleagues than for myself.

Early in my career as a journalist, I, too, obeyed the laws of "don't make waves." I, too, treaded water because I was the sole support of three children and had a job I loved doing—so why rock the boat for major promotions or hefty raises? Because of my—let's face it—fear of bringing untoward attention to myself, I remained silent and did my job, but I also missed out on opportunities to move ahead and for important assignments.

When I finally saw the light and began asking to be included in various projects, the response was one of surprise. My supervisors had not known what I was interested in. Once they knew and once I learned to ask for what I wanted, I got the opportunity to do something I had always wanted to do: write full-time about women's and employment issues.

··················· *Coach's Tip* ················

It's all wet to tread water.

··

Just as it's more than okay to get to work on time, stay late when necessary and offer to work overtime when it's appropriate, it's also more than okay to be alert to work that needs to be done and that you want to do. I think it's quite a compliment and not a put-down to be known as an "eager beaver."

Eager beavers are enthusiastic about the work they do because they have made sure they're doing something they love. Eager beavers have informal discussions now and then—but not too often—with their supervisors about what they see happening in the company and the roles they want to play in their department's success. Managers are human beings, too, and, if they have time, are willing to talk matters over with someone who clearly is deeply committed to doing the best job possible. Besides, the eager beaver makes the manager look good.

·················· *Coach's Tip* ··················

I'm rooting for you to be an eager beaver.

If the idea of informally "thrusting" yourself forward is something you just can't do—no matter how much you want to, no matter what the cost is to your career if you don't and even though your best friend, your coach, urges you to do so—there are other, more structured and socially acceptable ways to let it be known that you know what you want.

Most forward-looking companies have formal job postings for any openings that occur.

·················· *Coach's Tip* ··················

Apply for every job you're interested in—whether or not you have all the qualifications.

Applying for a job that's posted that you know you are in line for and deeply want is, of course, the correct and sanctioned way today to move ahead in a company. If you know you are a serious contender for the opening, I'm sure you'll have no qualms about applying. And when you do apply—after first announcing your intentions to do so by discussing it with your supervisor and the person whose name is on the job notice—I hope you get it. If not this time, you'll have better luck next time. That's what job posting is all about. But job posting also carries a secret agenda, and you can use it to your advantage.

"When I applied for the job of assistant financial manager at my company, I think everyone was in shock," said a sales representative at a large manufacturing company. "I was doing well in sales, but after three years I was getting burned out. My undergraduate degree is in business and I have a lot of smarts, so I applied—even though I knew I was a few credentials short."

He didn't get the job that time, but by applying for the promotion, he brought himself to the attention of management as a motivated candidate. Through the interviewing process, he also learned firsthand what he needed to qualify for that particular job.

"I saw what I needed was an MBA, and within a year I was accepted into the company's special graduate training program at a nearby university," he said. "I'm still working on getting my degree, and I'm still a sales rep—but I know when I complete the program, I'll be next in line for any opening in the financial department." And best of all, he says that by applying for the job, he got the attention of a well-respected manager in the financial in the department who now is his mentor.

· · · · · · · · · · · · · · · · · *Coach's Tip* · · · · · · · · · · · · · · · ·

Even if you're not completely qualified for the job you apply for, you'll be able to find out exactly what you need to make the grade next time. And now that your company knows what you want, it may help you acquire the skills you need.

· ·

Job posting gives you another advantage, too. It's a way of making known to your employer some important skills you already have that you haven't been able to utilize.

A large health-care association hired an excellent photographer with five years' experience to be chief photographer for their special publications. When the job of editor-in-chief for the organization became open, everyone was surprised—as they always are—when the photographer said that she intended to apply for the top job.

Her colleagues were skeptical—and so was management—that she could do a job that encompassed far more than photography. But she surprised them right back when she made her job application and resume into a well-edited, professional newsletter with an eye-catching layout, excellent headlines, good copy and, of course, quality photographs.

The stories in the "newsletter" recounted her experience, prizes and journalistic skills beyond photography. In both news and features stories, she explained that she was a journalism school graduate and had worked as a writer and editor as well as photographer for several small newspapers and magazines.

In other words, she proved, by actually doing it, that she could do everything the job demanded. She showed she had creativity and imagination—and that she could do the job. And she got it.

· · · · · · · · · · · · · · · · *Coach's Tip* · · · · · · · · · · · · · · ·

As you already know, I don't advise doing anything fancy with your resume when you're applying from outside the organization for a job. But when responding to jobs that are posted internally, use your creativity as an advantage.

· ·

Job posting is a wonderful tool that ensures all applicants an equal chance to be heard—not just the boss's favorites—and it also gives you a chance to communicate what you want and what you can do. And best of all, job posting makes everyone a player in the game of career success. It's an important mechanism in attracting and retaining a diverse workforce.

Another "sanctioned" time to speak up on your own behalf is during a performance review. Like job posting, most companies have instituted yearly *performance reviews*, an evaluation of the work you have done. They are held separately from salary reviews.

················· *Coach's Tip* ·················

P̲erformance reviews are especially important because at most companies you aren't eligible for a raise if you haven't had a performance review. And even if you don't anticipate your annual job review with joy and excitement, you certainly *do* want to qualify for a possible raise.

··

Your manager will notify you of your upcoming performance review. Usually you're given advance time to fill out a form that includes questions about how you rate your performance, professionalism and strongest contributions and strengths. You also get a chance to write down what you see as your areas for improvement and what your career objectives are. Finally, the last part of the form usually is for your supervisor's comments.

················· *Coach's Tip* ·················

O̲nce again, a performance review is no time to be modest. It's a discussion between two adults, although you must always keep in mind that one of you (the boss) is more equal than the other (you).

··

If you've done an excellent job in the past year, say so. If you've worked on a successful project, mention it. If you've brought positive attention to your department or to the company in some way, write it down. If you've worked long hours, mentored another employee, volunteered for special activities, now's the time to list them.

The overall evaluation of your work is made by your supervisor. Together, you discuss your strengths and weaknesses, but it is the supervisor's unilateral opinion—not yours—that goes into the final performance review, the one that goes into your personnel record.

The performance review is a powerful professional tool, and you get to use it only once a year, so take your time filling out the form given to you by your supervisor before your discussion. Be prepared to state your case clearly and with conviction during the actual review with your manager.

If you work as a team, check with other team members about what they think the most important things are that you achieved as a group in the past year. Ask them what they consider your personal contributions—and when you fill in the review form, mention that your teammates think this is what you have done exceptionally well.

· · · · · · · · · · · · · · · · · *Coach's Tip* · · · · · · · · · · · · · · · ·

If I were there at the performance review, behind that closed door in the boss's office, I would tell your supervisor for you what an asset you are to the staff. Since I can't be there, you are the only one who can speak up for yourself. So do it!

· ·

It's up to you to make sure your manager gives you a precise and definite review, one not sprinkled with vague generalities. For instance, if your boss says that your work in one area "needs improvement," find out exactly what that means. Ask if you need to be more productive; if that's the problem, how productive? Ask for real numbers and goals.

If your boss refers to a personality conflict between you and a co-worker, ask for the specific situation. Get everything out in the open. Make sure you know what your supervisor thinks you did wrong and exactly what you should do about it.

· · · · · · · · · · · · · · · · · *Coach's Tip* · · · · · · · · · · · · · · · ·

Asking for specific examples or trying to pin your manager down to the exact facts would be considered too confrontational in any situation other than a performance review.

· ·

A review is set up to get all the necessary job-related information out on the table and to make sure there is no misunderstanding between you or your supervisor about how you are doing. An honest discussion of your work and how you measure up to your manager's expectations are the stated aims of an evaluation of your professional performance. But there's more to work reviews than meets the eye, just as there is to job posting.

On most evaluation forms, one of the most important topics listed for mutual discussion is "employee's career objectives." Even if it's not spelled out on the form, a performance review is the perfect time to bring up the subject of what you, in your heart of hearts, really want—without fear of being pushy or too demanding. This is what you've been getting in shape for all these months. Your employer actually wants to know what you want.

Remember, performance reviews now are much more goal-related than they were before the massive downsizings and restructuring of corporate America. The same ground rules apply to salary reviews: Nothing is a given. If you don't perform well, there's a strong possibility you may not get a raise at all.

· · · · · · · · · · · · · · · · *Coach's Tip* · · · · · · · · · · · · · · · ·

Sell yourself well in your performance review, and then six months later, when you have your annual salary review, sell yourself again.

· ·

People used to work all their lives for one company, and their raises were automatic. Not anymore. With companies looking to get the most production possible from each employee, automatic raises have gone the way of seniority as the basis for promotion.

· · · · · · · · · · · · · · · · *Coach's Tip* · · · · · · · · · · · · · · · ·

Good raises are given only if you earn them.

· ·

The frustrating news for some employees is that companies these days, those that are not unionized, can and do institute salary freezes whenever they think it's necessary to do so—even though the CEO and other top executives continue to get enormous increases, stock options and other financial perks.

But you can't give up your efforts to earn the wages you should be making. Instead, you must be aware that longevity has nothing to do with getting a 5 percent raise. The main factor at work in determining who gets what is *pay for performance.*

··············· *Coach's Tip* ···············

Those the company considers its "A" players will get the best increases.

··

If you're within a certain salary grade, you know your parameters from the beginning. You're not going to get a raise that takes you out of your job classification, but you do want to move up in it. Before your salary review, ask your manager or supervisor to see your company's salary grades and classifications. Let the grades be a guide to what you can possibly ask for and possibly get. Keep your request for a raise within the boundaries of your category. Otherwise, you'll just be spinning your wheels.

More homework: It's back to the books—and annual statements—to check on your company's financial condition. What do analysts think of your company's future? Has the company been laying off people recently, or does it have plans to do so? Ask around in other parts of your company to find out how important your department's work is considered to be in the overall picture. You may not like what you learn because, of course, you know you're an excellent worker and deserve to be compensated for your efforts.

And the well-toned employees in the top echelons of the company are vulnerable to downsizing as well. Asking for too high a raise may turn out to be a severe muscle cramp in your efforts to make known what you want, move ahead and, ultimately, make Big Bucks.

················ *Coach's Tip* ················

Talking about salary "negotiations" for many employees is a moot point because most raises are predetermined—and there's little you can do about them.

···

"I went into my boss's office, anticipating a really good discussion, and what I was told was that I was getting a 3 percent raise, they'd try to do better next year—but that was it," an office manager said. "It was depressing, but there was nothing I could do about it."

She was right. There was nothing she could do about the raise itself. Managers are telling employees that they have only a lump sum of money, that it's a very small amount and if they increase your raise, they'll have to take something away from someone else in the department. Managers usually try to use whatever funds they have to bring up the salaries of those who are severely underpaid and to reward only the very top performers.

Even though it won't change this year's raise—they're usually written in stone—make clear to your supervisor how disappointed you are. Say that you want to be considered for a much larger raise next year. And tell your manager, in a businesslike and nonconfrontational way, that you plan to discuss your salary with the human resources department and the executive in charge of your department. Then, do both.

················ *Coach's Tip* ················

But when you do have some leverage, some room to play around in, state your case firmly.

···

Now is the time to remind your manager of your accomplishments, the good work you've done or the new project you created and completed that brought thousands of dollars into the company. Now is the time to say you want to be in an equal pay position with your colleagues; otherwise, you will continue to lag behind and will never catch up.

·················   *Coach's Tip*   ·················

If you are a new hire and did not get the salary you thought you deserved when you started your job, remind your manager of the fact.

···

Point out how quickly you've learned the work, how well you fit into the corporate culture and how eager you are to contribute more. List for your manager the new projects you have in mind and how they will increase your value to the company.

·················   *Coach's Tip*   ·················

Salary reviews are not supposed to be performance reviews, but unless you are willing to take whatever is given you and leave quietly, you should use this opportunity to remind your boss of your contributions.

···

Secretaries and other support staff face a barrier that most others do not. They're paid not for their responsibilities or contributions to the company, but their wages instead are usually determined by the rank of the person for whom they work. Since most support staff and secretaries are women, this is a form of sex discrimination that the federal Equal Pay Act doesn't cover.

The Equal Pay Act ensures that everyone doing the same job gets the same pay. It doesn't apply to secretaries' salaries because 90 percent are female and most get the same low pay. I urge secretaries and other support staff to campaign hard and long for passage of *pay equity* or *comparable worth laws*. Pay equity ensures that you get paid for what you do and are not penalized for your gender, race or the status of the person you report to.

If you know how much of a raise you deserve and you get it—that's cause for celebration. But if more money is not coming your way at least for a year or salaries are frozen, you can ask for and possibly receive other things. Here are some things to ask for:

- A bonus. It's a one-time reward and is not part of your annual salary. If you already are on bonus, now is the time to ask for a higher one. And if you're at the top end of your salary category—with no promotion in sight—asking for a bonus is appropriate.

- More vacation days

- Opportunities to attend workshops, conferences and seminars in your field

- The company to pay for subscriptions for you to professional magazines and newsletters

- To be included in special department projects

·············· *Coach's Tip* ··············

Never threaten to quit if you don't get what you want—even if you do intend to leave. Keep your cool.
··

To remain professional during salary discussions, remember that some people are getting salary reductions instead of raises. And the truth is that you can start looking elsewhere if you feel the money door has slammed shut on you. Meanwhile, you have another year to gather your strength and present your case again.

"I thought I'd never be able to make any more money," a reader told me. "I was stuck at 3 percent raises each year, which kept me up with inflation and nothing more. But I hung in there at my salary and performance reviews; I continued to let my boss know how serious and ambitious I am. And it paid off after five years." The way it paid off was that the reader was finally promoted to a new job, and the salary increase amounted to 10 percent!

·················· *Coach's Tip* ················

Whatever works is good.

···

Now that you've limbered yourself up by letting people know what you want, the next step is to make it happen—by taking personal charge of your career.

PART THREE

Taking Charge
of Your Career

·····11·····

Only You Care about Your Career

It's kind of a lonely thought to think that you are the only one in the world who cares about your career. As a matter of fact, I, as your coach, care about it, too—a lot. In that sense you're not completely alone in your efforts to have a happy and successful career.

················· *Coach's Tip* ·················

But you are the only one who can make things happen over the course of your working life. You are the only one in charge of your career.

··

One of the subjects I get asked about almost as often as I do about resumes is the importance of having a strategy, a specific goal, a five-year plan. "Do I need to sit down and plan exactly where I hope to be in five years, what my title will be and how much I'll be making?" a reader asks. "It sounds like a good exercise, but the thought of doing so is overwhelming."

Plotting the graph of the next few years of your professional life helps you focus your career and come to grips with reality. It's obvious that deciding on the steps in the ladder of upward job mobility can't do a lot of harm. The problem is that the labor market is so volatile today that while writing down your plan isn't a bad idea, sticking to it may not be possible.

A disadvantage of creating a strict plan you intend to adhere to no matter what is that you can't factor in change. And change, flexibility and transition are the buzzwords of employment in the 21st century.

··················· *Coach's Tip* ···················

Don't set yourself up for defeat, frustration or self-recrimination. Look at your plan for the future as a blueprint for a dream house you'd really like to build someday, if everything goes well.

My five-year plan always has been to get through tomorrow, so you can see immediately that I don't take very seriously the calisthenics involved in planning a rigid outline of long-term job strategies—no matter how enthusiastic the yuppies were about them in the 1980s. However, as I emphasized in Chapter 9, I do advise planning ahead every moment of your workday and week.

··················· *Coach's Tip* ···················

It's important to know where you want to go so that, hopefully, you can get there. But don't let your list of career goals and timetables get in the way of your success.

To spell out graphically the promotions you hope to get and the advances you hope to make, you must sit down and figure out what your next step upward and the ones after that should be—and the process itself will give you some very important information about what your future may be.

Here are the times when having a formal, written plan is a helpful exercise—as long as you don't lock yourself into it regardless of changes in your work and personal life:

- When you are graduated from high school, a training program or from college

- When you start a new job or assignment

- When you decide that you need more education and enroll for advanced training or degrees

- When, as a mature adult, you plan to enter the workforce for the first time

- If you plan to reenter the workforce after a long absence

- If you're thinking about changing jobs or starting your own business

················ *Coach's Tip* ·················

Write down how you see yourself advancing, and look at it from time to time. Use your plan as a suggestion, not a command.

··

Some goal-oriented people list not only the position they expect to be holding over the next few years, but they also list the salary they want to make. I think it's important to have a handle on what you *should* be making—which often is different from what you *want* to make.

A pleasant maxim is that you should make at least $1,000 a year more than your age, so that at age 21, you'd make $22,000 and at age 65, $66,000. It's important to have salary goals, as long as they're realistic, because often they serve as incentives for doing better.

·················· *Coach's Tip* ·················

Look at the salaries you project for yourself as parameters of what you think you will be worth to your employer. If you don't reach them at the time you hoped to, don't despair. At least you still have a job.

·····································

Wages will not increase in the next decade; in fact, many salaries will decline. So if you do have a formalized plan for the future of your career, you might be smart not to emphasize salary too much or to leave it out completely.

Being in charge of your career means more than having a plan. It means making sure that you don't stay in one job too long or at one level forever. Some people measure success by a promotion at least every two years, but in practicality it varies according to what you do and where you work.

Two years is a short period of time for advancement if, for instance, you're a lawyer and your goal is to become a partner; if you're a gofer at an advertising agency and see your next move up is to account assistant, two years is an eternity. Since so many people are starting jobs at the bottom of the career ladder—instead of somewhere in the middle—the good news is that the only way to go is up. And the next good news is that you *can* make that next step happen.

It's a truism that the opportunities to move up from the lower levels are far more numerous than those for employees in the middle. But it's also true that not everyone moves up.

It does happen occasionally that some people are snatched up from the lower ranks to high posts they never applied for, much to their delight. Often they deserve such recognition and are lucky to be singled out. More often, those who are chosen in this manner are related to someone high up or have some other personal connection with those in power.

················ *Coach's Tip* ················

For the rest of us working stiffs, we have to do it our-
selves: Only highly motivated people who don't wait to be
offered a good opportunity or assignment but create their
own openings are the ones who move ahead.

···

Whether you're a fast-food cook, an administrative assistant,
a telemarketing associate, an entry-level automobile mechanic, a
hospital aide or retail or marketing trainee, it's up to you to care
enough about your career to get to the very next best step.

If you are in a relatively entry-level position, here's how to
stand out from the crowd of people at the same level:

- Ask a lot of questions. That doesn't mean you should be a
  pain in the neck. It does mean you should ask enough
  questions to be able to do your present job well.

- Do your present job well.

- Volunteer for new assignments and projects.

- Be a team player, even if you don't belong to a specific
  team.

- Join professional organizations and other groups connected with your work. Such groups will advance your
  personal and your professional goals.

- Get a mentor. (See Chapter 9.)

- Watch carefully for job openings that are posted. (See
  Chapter 10.)

Job postings are an invaluable tool for knowing what positions
are available and for letting the company know that *you* are available for the next notch up. Apply for any job posted that is close
to what you want and that your skills come close to matching.

Pick a role model, preferably among your colleagues or
superiors—someone who has been able to move ahead within a
reasonable period of time. Try to emulate the moves this person
has made.

················· *Coach's Tip* ················

If you can't find a role model nearby, seek out talented people among your contacts outside the office.
··

The previous advice is geared to entry-level workers of all ages, but it also applies to experienced, long-term employees. But *senior employees*—a term that describes anyone who's been on the payroll for five years or more—have some problems and options the new kids on the block do not.

················· *Coach's Tip* ················

Mature baby boomers, the majority of the workforce, will be tripping all over each other to get the few promotions or management slots that will be open to them.
··

The advantage of having been on board for a few years is that you know firsthand the lay of the land, who can help you move ahead, who wants to keep you back, what turns your boss on and off and what direction the company is going in. At least, you *should* know by then!

It's essential for long-term employees to keep doing their homework—or, to mix a metaphor, keep their ears to the ground to see which way the wind is blowing. Seasoned workers also must keep applying for jobs, posted and unposted, instead of waiting to be asked. If you feel that you've been passed over once too often, ask your boss what's happening. Are you at a standstill, and if so, what can you do about it?

The advantage employees with experience have is that if the climb upward is temporarily blocked or clogged with too many competitors, they can always move sideways, or laterally. As Mary Ann Jirak of Harper College Career Transition Center suggests, "Consider multiple futures! Contemplate a career in a horizontal context rather than a vertical one."

Though *multiple, horizontal* and *vertical* are words with sexual overtones, Jirak is actually referring only to *lateral moves*, transfers at the same level either within your department or to another department in the company. Although your job classification remains at the same level, these moves often involve a slight increase in salary, just to sweeten the pot.

················· *Coach's Tip* ·················

The route to success no longer is straight up. It zigzags. The more experience you have and the greater your awareness of how the company is run, the better your chance to move ahead.

··

Even after you get one promotion, you can't sit back on your laurels—unless you always want to stay where you are. But even standing still isn't an option: If you become stagnant or indifferent to the progress of your career, you will be the first one to be replaced by a smart machine or simply let go.

················· *Coach's Tip* ·················

Every day at work is an audition for your next promotion or your next job.

··

Here are some prescriptions for taking charge of your career on a daily basis:

- *Volunteer for special projects.* If you're not invited to work on the projects you want to be a part of or are consistently left out, come up with ideas for projects that you know the company needs to start. Sell your idea to your manager, after getting support for it from your colleagues.

  It will be hard to leave you off an important project that *you* dreamed up!

- *Volunteer for companywide task forces.* Usually anyone who is interested is allowed to serve on these committees that do everything from decide what computer system your company should install to what changes need to be made in the cafeteria. They require a lot of hard work and long hours.

Every task force you're on—especially those devoted to studying and coming up with recommendations on "delicate" issues such as implementing diversity, ethics policies and new ways of getting the job done—gives you visibility. And visibility sheds positive light on your career.

- *Be active in community activities and professional organizations.* If you can't get the visibility you need within the company, go outside. Be active in community groups— and report your volunteer achievements to your manager and to your company newsletter. Coach an amateur team, give talks at schools and colleges, work on a committee for a professional organization, head a neighborhood drive or be active in community theater. You'll enjoy it, and it all pays off. (See Chapter 19.)

·············· *Coach's Tip* ················

Be as cooperative as possible in helping a new idea, project or department get off the ground. Even if you're not directly involved in it, volunteer to help out or be supportive of the people working on it.

··

A major food company prepared to launch a new product at supermarkets throughout the country. It chose a Saturday as the date to inundate stores with the new brand, a culmination of three years of expensive research and marketing tests.

"I saw a sign posted asking for people willing to work locally that Saturday to help market the product," said a woman who was employed in the giant firm's corporate headquarters. "I was an administrator in the finance department, and the note was aimed more at support staff, but I wanted to do something to rekindle the company's interest in me—which seemed to be dead for too long. And, truthfully, I really wanted to do something to show how much I care about the company and to be part of the team."

She worked on that project and on the next few projects, too. At training sessions for company volunteer marketers, she met top-ranking corporate officials who vaguely knew of her existence and were surprised to see her. They asked what she was doing there and why she was sacrificing her time off. Her reply was, "I know how important it is for this product to be a success, and I want to help."

She said the experience was serendipitous because she worked side by side with people at every level of the company, people she had not known before and who became her friends. And another happy result was that one of the top executives she had worked with, side by side as a volunteer, asked if she would mind coming to work for his department. She didn't mind one bit! "I have the same title and got only a small raise, but I know that now I'm viewed as a serious player in moving ahead in this company," she said.

·················· *Coach's Tip* ·················

Be a serious player.

··

Doing your work well, making sure everyone knows that you're eager to move ahead and being highly visible are the basic underpinnings of taking charge of your career. But some workers have special problems that can be viewed as obstacles or as challenges.

I prefer to view them as challenges.

Working from home is a wonderful opportunity, made possible by our high-tech, automated society. But not being at the worksite on a regular basis hurts your visibility.

·················· *Coach's Tip* ·················

If you work from home, go to the office one day a week. Show up for important meetings. Always be available if you're needed.

··

Working overseas is a coveted assignment, but unfortunately you may be forgotten, especially when the big promotions open up. Some 250,000 U.S. employees worked abroad in 1994, and they, too, must be in charge of their careers.

·················· *Coach's Tip* ················

Keep in constant touch with your home office. Send faxes and E-mail about your accomplishments—even before you put them in your formal reports. Ask your colleagues at the home office to keep you advised of what's happening in the trenches.
··

And when you return for meetings or even vacations, spend most of your time at headquarters, nosing around for information and maintaining friendships. Obstacles and challenges can be overcome if all things are equal, but frequently all things are not equal.

Discrimination often hampers women and minorities from moving ahead according to their ability. Secretaries, 90 percent of whom are women, in particular, are blocked from moving out of the ranks of support personnel. A white male hired as a mail clerk or administrative assistant has a chance to move ahead, but most women secretaries are firmly locked into their jobs.

·················· *Coach's Tip* ················

Being constantly passed over for promotion when you are a qualified candidate is against the law, but secretaries, like everyone else, must apply for every job opening that occurs—and who knows first or better than secretaries what jobs will be open?
··

You must also show how serious you are about your career by asking your manager to send you to special workshops—e.g., for computer training and advanced degrees.

It's especially important for women and minorities to tell their supervisors that they want to move ahead. Otherwise it will be convenient to forget them. The *glass ceiling* describes the artificial barriers that keep women and minorities from good assignments and good promotions, but it is not imaginary. It's real.

It's so real, in fact, that the first federal "glass ceiling" case, recently announced by the U.S. Department of Labor, resulted in a $603,943 settlement that Fairfax Hospital in Falls Church, Virginia, must pay 52 women stuck at close-to-the-top management positions at the hospital. The settlement benefits all female and minority employees at the hospital.

·················· *Coach's Tip* ················

Keep careful records of alleged discrimination against you, especially in promotions. Sometimes the only way to put a dent in the glass ceiling is to file a lawsuit with local, state or federal antidiscrimination agencies.

··

Here are some more tips for women and minorities hitting up against the glass ceiling:

- Speak up at meetings. Then send a memo to those who attend about what your suggestions are so that no one else takes credit for them.

- Create your own support group with other women and minorities to strategize effective ways of advancing your careers.

An Asian American woman told me she was so tired of being ignored at staff meetings that she wore a clown's nose that lit up to one of the meetings. When she had something to say, she blinked the light. It worked. She never had to do it again.

Another important facet of being in charge of your career is recognizing when, no matter what you do, you aren't getting anywhere in your present job. You're excluded from important meetings and decisions, you haven't gotten a good raise in years, you're at the top of your salary range with nowhere to go, you're turned down for lateral moves and you no longer feel that you're much of a contributor—even though you want to be.

•••••••••••••••••• *Coach's Tip* ••••••••••••••••••

Pay attention to those inner voices. This is called "listening with your third ear," which refers to our intuition, a sixth sense that we cannot ignore. Another phrase for it is "that sinking feeling."

••

What it adds up to is that you've stayed in your present job too long. It's time to polish up your resume, start making contacts and look for another job. (See Chapter 2.)

•••••••••••••••••• *Coach's Tip* ••••••••••••••••••

Even if you think the economic times are too harsh to start a job search, you probably have no choice. All the signs are there; leave before you're fired.

••

If you don't move fast enough or are taken by surprise, your career coach will give you some tips in the next chapter about what to do if you're fired.

12

What To Do
If You're Fired

Being fired is a nightmare you never wanted to happen, especially to you and especially if it comes as a shock. No matter whether it's labeled an outright, old-fashioned firing or layoff or is modernized into being a downsizing or right-structuring, it still hurts.

If you expected to be let go, perhaps you are somewhat mentally prepared to handle the situation and are ready to do the hard work that comes next to become reemployed. And if you hated your job, you probably had feelers out for a new one, or at best, you were not taken by surprise.

The surprise and embarrassment hurt as much as losing a steady income and a place to go every day. Yet what always surprises *me* is how often people say, "It was a rotten, unfair thing, being fired, but I always hated my job anyway."

················ *Coach's Tip* ················

Surprised or not, ready or not, you're going to have to start a job search all over again. (See Chapters 1 through 5.) But before you start a new job hunt, prepare yourself for an exit from the company that is dignified and practical. You will have to foresee and tie up every detail in advance of your leaving that will help and protect you in the future and in your new job.

••

So limber up your career muscles with these tips to help you get started on that important assignment:

- *Understand that the word* fired *no longer is the "f" word it once was.* It is nothing to be ashamed of. It is nothing to hide. You are not damaged goods. Merger mania in the 1980s forced out middle managers, and restructuring in the 1990s eliminated everyone else who could be erased. Today most people understand that employers are cutting staff wherever they can—even perfectly capable, qualified people. Even you.

- *Ask for a complete explanation of why you were let go.* You have nothing to lose, and the information is essential. Also ask if you have any chance of being rehired in the future. Try to get your manager to level with you.

- *Analyze for yourself why you were fired.* Was it more than just a staff reduction, and if so, why you? When you figure out why this low blow was delivered, you'll be much better prepared to avoid the same situation in the future—if it's something within your control and not purely due to the company's financial difficulties.

- *If you were taken by surprise, now is the time to figure out what you failed to notice.* And if you weren't surprised to be discharged but were shocked at the timing, what clues did you ignore? Some typical signs of impending doom are poor performance, lack of promotions, absence of salary increases and being left out of important projects. (See Chapter 10.) Some typical signs of budget troubles at your company are previous cutbacks in staff, financial officers who attend huddled meetings on the weekends, poor performance of the company and negative reports on the company in financial publications, newspapers and professional magazines.

- *Consult an employment lawyer if you think you may be a victim of discrimination.* And no matter what your level is, it's important to discuss your firing with a lawyer so that you leave with everything you are entitled to, know what to ask for and have legal protection if you don't get what rightfully is yours.

- *Don't panic.* This is a very hard moment in your life, but it's not exactly the same as being in an airplane crash or being diagnosed with a terminal disease—even if it feels that way. You will survive, and you will be okay. You'll probably be even happier in your next job.

- *Recognize that being fired is a serious crisis in your life that will eventually pass and be forgotten.* In the interim, while you're closing down at your former job and getting ready to find the next one, be very nice to yourself. I advise lots of sex or lots of chocolate bars (large chocolate bars, not the small ones, and with almonds).

················· *Coach's Tip* ················

Formulate in your mind an exit strategy. Prepare for your negotiations with your supervisor or personnel department. Talk to a lawyer. Write down exactly what you want from the company. Don't miss a detail.

·····································

And line up whatever powerful allies you may have in the company who will help you leave with your pockets full, rather than half-empty. They also will give you good references.

"I saw the ax coming," a former data processing manager told me. "I admit I was into denial for a long time, but when I began to acknowledge how much of our work was being outsourced, I knew I had to do something to defend myself. I wasn't quite up to putting out feelers for another job, but I did start talking to top managers about the fact that if my department were eliminated, I would like to start my own consulting business—and I wanted the company's account. I reminded them that no one knows the work better than I do and that no one else is so familiar with its procedures."

And it worked. When the entire department was shut down a few months later, she was able to take a lot of the work with her. "My former employer was my first account," she said. "The company still had contracts with other consultants, but as they ended, I got the business. And the only reason I got the account in the first place was that I moved early and had friends in high places. They couldn't save my job, but they could give me a big boost in becoming an independent consultant."

Now that you've stopped reeling—at least a little—from the shock of actually losing your job, have found out why you were fired and have tried to enlist the support of powerful friends in the firm, the next step you must take is to *make a deal*. In other words, get ready to negotiate your exit.

················ *Coach's Tip* ················

To stretch your muscles to prepare for negotiations with your soon-to-be former employer, you have some serious homework to do. You probably will be offered the standard exit package of salary, health benefits and pension benefits, but if you know what to ask for, you may get a sweeter deal.

··

Remember, whatever you do get is small potatoes compared to losing a career.

Here are some steps to take even before you figure out what it is you want from the company:

- Get a lawyer.

- If your company has an employee handbook, read it carefully. Make sure every step was followed as outlined, that you were given proper warning and are being offered exactly what you should be getting.

- *Employment at will* is a favorite buzzword in human resources departments, especially at times of firing. This means that the company legally can dismiss you at any time for any reason. Employees who belong to unions or who work in states that do not allow employment at will cannot be so easily dismissed. However, if your employer does invoke "employment at will" when firing you, check the handbook and make certain that it's spelled out. If it isn't, you may have the basis of a lawsuit, as oral statements don't constitute company policy.

- *Full financial disclosure* is a legal requisite of employers who are asked how the company is doing by job candidates during the hiring process. If you were lied to about the condition of the company and are being let go because it is doing poorly, once again you have grounds for a lawsuit.

- *Wrongful discharge* is another basis for a lawsuit. If you've been fired for allegedly committing a crime that you are not guilty of and it has not been proven, yet again you have legal recourse. Wrongful discharge is especially important to follow up on because the charges will follow you the rest of your professional and personal life.

·················· *Coach's Tip* ··················

The more ammunition you have and the more facts you have about your rights, the stronger will be your performance in the play-offs of your final negotiations.

··

Go to your negotiating meeting with confidence. Once again, it's no time to be confrontational or bitter. Be professional, as always. With the help of your lawyer, you know what's possible to ask for beyond the ordinary. You've done your homework and have found out what other people are getting.

Your coach also has some advice for you about what to ask for. And even if you're turned down, you don't lose anything by asking.

- *Ask for a letter of reference to be given to you on your last day.* You want to take it with you. You don't want to be held hostage by the company for any reason whatsoever for a reference letter after you leave.

- *If the company says that you must leave immediately or in two weeks, try to get more time.* Time is money at this point, because your severance pay can't start until you actually leave. And any time you get will give you a leg up on your job search.

- *Offer to train your replacement, if there is one.* Offer to finish up any projects you're working on or to explain where you are in them to your supervisor or colleagues. Your offer may be refused, but it's the professional thing to do. And if it's accepted, that also gives you more time.

- *Severance pay varies as to your length of service and the size of the company.* It usually is at least a week's pay for every year of service plus any unused vacation time or days due. Assuming that's what you'll be offered, figure out in advance exactly what that number is. You don't want to be taken advantage of.

- *No matter what level you're at, if you feel your severance package isn't enough compensation for the hard work you've done for the company and your long years of service, ask for a bonus at the end of the severance period.* You just might get it, even though the company knows you will be getting unemployment compensation—which it has contributed to.

- *Make sure that you clearly understand how long your health benefits will last.* Ask your company to keep you in their health plan if you don't find a job before your benefits expire. Offer to pay whatever the cost will be to remain in it.

- *Discuss the tax implications of severance pay, benefits and pensions, and try to work out a payment schedule that will work best for you.* If you're talking about substantial sums of money, check out the numbers with an accountant or with your lawyer. Remember that *severance pay* is taxable income unless it's payment for damages, such as those from wrongful discharge, settlement of personal injury or discrimination cases.

- *Ask for outplacement services.* An outplacement organization is hired by former employers to counsel fired or laid-off employees in job-hunting techniques. Outplacement agencies do not find people jobs, but they are invaluable in helping you move in the right direction toward a new one, polishing up your resume, getting job tips and getting the emotional support that both you and your family may need. Outplacement agencies also give you an office address and telephone number to work out of and to use in your job search.

- *If the company turns you down for outplacement, ask whether you can use an empty desk or office with a telephone to pursue your next job.* Companies will not do this for people they don't want around, but often they are amenable to this arrangement in cases of massive layoffs.

- *Find out if your company has any programs to help workers in transition—in other words, those on their way out.* Some companies give workshops and seminars in-house that offer career counseling, resume writing, interviewing skills and advice on how to start your own business. You want to be able to take advantage of whatever resources the company has.

- *Hold off signing any documents until your lawyer reviews them.* At the end of your negotiations (which, hopefully, will be extremely profitable), you will be asked to sign papers. Even though you are told—and you will be—that you will not get anything from the company, including a reference, until you do so, *don't sign anything.* Make sure that your lawyer goes over the papers first, especially if they include clauses that limit you from working in any area of your profession for a specific amount of years or forbid you to file suit for damages of any kind.

·················· *Coach's Tip* ··················

Even after you get your lawyer's okay, take your time about signing those papers. Make sure that you are as comfortable with them as you can be, under the circumstances.

···

The negotiations were rough, but you survived them. How-ever, you're not completely out of there. You still have the exit interview.

The exit interview usually is conducted by the human re-source department, not your manager. It's the time you're sup-posed to say how you feel about the company and the way it works. It's also a "good" time to get even with everyone who you think has wronged you—or is it?

·················· *Coach's Tip* ··················

Don't be tempted by revenge. Unless you know of some stealing going on or other unethical behavior that directly affected you and may have led to your dismissal, be nice. It won't hurt.

··

Most people feel that they have no obligation to the people who are getting rid of them to give them inside tips on how the company really should be run. I agree. In my mind, exit inter-views are comparable to the fox asking Red Riding Hood to sug-gest better ways of abducting young girls. Forget it—unless you really want to get off your chest something that will make you feel better about yourself and your experiences working for the company.

Well, you've lived through the ordeals of negotiating the best severance deal possible and of faking the exit interview. Now's the time to think about what to do next.

·················· *Coach's Tip* ··················

If you have a window of opportunity, take a little time off just to relax and do whatever you want. Of course, you're not going to forget for one minute that you've been fired, but you do need a little time to recuperate before going back into the fray.

··

I'm not suggesting an expensive vacation to a sunny island, though it's a wonderful idea if you can afford it. I'm just pointing out that this is a very good time to kick back, take it easy, be nice to your family and friends who have put up with you without a complaint throughout this ordeal—and take stock of your life.

·············· *Coach's Tip* ················

Use your down time to figure out what you enjoy doing. And if you don't enjoy what you're doing now, consider a career switch.

··

"I hate that I had to give up my job, but I did take enough time to sit down and figure out what I really wanted to do—and it was something else," said a hospital administrator who lost his job when the institution was merged with a much larger chain of hospitals. By doing what is called "examining your navel," he discovered that what he liked best about his job was helping others, and that led him to apply for a job he knew was open as executive director of a nonprofit social service agency. The pay was less, but so was the stress. "If I hadn't taken a little bit of time to analyze how I felt about being fired and where I wanted to go, I might have ended up in the same exact situation I had been in before," he said. Don't repeat your previous mistakes in your search for a new job. You're starting with a clean slate.

Analyze what skills you have that are transferable to a new field if you feel that your current profession offers few opportunities. This is easier to do if you hated your previous job, but even if you loved it, now is the time to be realistic.

·············· *Coach's Tip* ················

Hedge your bets by going back to the library and doing your homework to find out where the jobs actually are, both by industry and by geographical location.

··

As I've often stressed, the service-producing sector of the U.S. economy is the place to look for jobs for the 1990s and well into the next century. The service-producing sector includes transportation, travel and hospitality, communications, utilities, wholesale and retail trade, finance, insurance, real estate, government and the service industry. The latter includes business services, such as lawyers, accountants and court reporters; health-care and personal services; automotive services; legal and educational services; and social services.

If you're mobile—and you have to be able to pick up and move to work anywhere in the country or in the world—think about going to the South or to the West to look for a job. States such as Utah, Nevada, Colorado and New Mexico are creating jobs at a rapid rate. So are Florida, Georgia and Texas. All seven of these states are expected to maintain that growth throughout the decade.

················ *Coach's Tip* ················

It's costly to be unemployed, and it's also costly to hunt for a job. But job-hunting costs are tax deductible, often even if you don't get the job. So keep a careful record of every expenditure you make, including phone calls, stationery, stamps, transportation, professional counseling and any miscellaneous expenses (including chocolate bars, though the IRS may not accept them as a legitimate job-hunting expense).

···

As I warned you earlier in the chapters when I coached you on how to get the right job—and everything that I said then applies to you now—it's going to take a while to find a new job. And if you had a very good one, it will take you even longer.

Budget your severance pay and unemployment compensation to get you through the next few months—that's what they're for. Make sure you'll have enough money for the long haul, because you don't want to be pressured by a lack of sufficient income to take a job you don't like or that isn't right for you. Otherwise you may be back on the street looking again in a short period of time. And who wants to do that?

················· *Coach's Tip* ·················

Move slowly and cautiously when looking for a job after being fired. It's a situation that is best compared to being jilted by someone you really loved very much. You don't want to take a new job on the rebound, just to prove to the world that you are employable.

···

You know you have skills and abilities that employers want. Remember all you have to offer when you're on your new job hunt. Don't be defensive in job interviews; you haven't done anything wrong. In fact, you've done a lot of things right.

················· *Coach's Tip* ·················

Whatever you do, don't immediately take the first job you're offered.

···

It may be extremely gratifying to be offered a job after suffering through what you considered the humiliation of being discharged. But proceed carefully. Make sure it's the job you want. If it isn't right for you, there will be others.

All it takes is hard work.

When you finally do land your next job—and you will land one—never forget for even one moment that you might lose your job yet again, even through no fault of your own.

That's why it's so important for every career-minded person to learn how to network, to make the needed contacts to advance in your profession and bounce back from defeat. In the next chapter I'll tell you everything you ever wanted to know about networking.

13

Networking Every Possible Connection

 Webster's *New World Dictionary* defines the noun *network* in two ways:

1. Any arrangement of fabrics or parallel wires, threads, etc., crossed at regular intervals by others fastened to them so as to have open spaces.

2. A system of interconnected or cooperating individuals.

They are the official definitions, and both apply to the kind of networking I'm referring to, namely, individuals joining together to help themselves and others move ahead.

Within that context, here's my personal description of what *networking*, the verb, really is all about: It's not only what you know, it's who you know. (Or, for the purists, *whom* you know.)

This means being part of an informal group, such as networking with trusted colleagues at lunchtime or belonging to a formal organization, such as the American Management Association, which has local chapters, annual meetings, professional publications and seminars. Belonging to a network helps you gain power and influence in the world of business.

··············· *Coach's Tip* ···············

To keep up to date in your field, to advance your career and to know everything that's happening or going to happen in the workplace—network, network, network.

··

The success of networks and the individuals in them can be traced to an old law of physics: The whole is greater than the sum of its parts. In Chicago, where we are very savvy about such matters, we call it "clout."

Another way to look at networking is this: The sound of one hand clapping doesn't make much noise.

··············· *Coach's Tip* ···············

Don't expect a network to produce results for you immediately. First you have to pay your dues.

··

You can't show up at your first meeting of your new network or professional organization and immediately start asking people to tell you all the inside information they know to help you advance in your career. Instead, show your commitment to the group and its individual members by volunteering to help the network in whatever way you can and by showing your eagerness to share information.

Even though you may not have anything new to report about what's going on in your company, you may have helpful information that you've learned about other firms or other professions.

··············· *Coach's Tip* ···············

Networking does not mean telling everyone about information that is helpful to you personally, such as an important job opening you are interested in.

··

It's counterproductive for you to give away inside tips and other information that might limit your own opportunities. In fact, it's crazy, and it's not what networking is about; no one expects you to do anything so foolish. But if there's a job opening you're not interested in, announce it. If there's a consulting contract that you've turned down for some reason, inform your network members. If you've heard of a firm's plans to let people go, that's the kind of information to share.

With almost half of all jobs attained through personal contacts—which is a low estimate, in my opinion—you need a network just to keep you and your job on an even playing field.

·················· *Coach's Tip* ··················

Once you're established in your group, network every chance you can by asking for information and giving it, too.

···

Don't confine your networking to structured meetings or organizations, though they are extremely important avenues of job-related information.

Here is your coach's list of other places to network:

- After work
- Airplanes
- Bars
- Community groups
- Elevators
- Escalators
- Golf courses
- Locker rooms
- Power breakfasts
- Power dinners
- Power lunches

- Private clubs

- Tennis courts

- Volunteer groups

- Washrooms

- Work

·············· *Coach's Tip* ················

Networks are springboards. Use them to leverage power and control over your career.
···

How do networks differ from volunteer groups, clubs, unions, community groups and most other forms of organized activities? The differences are exactly what make networks so attractive, so necessary and so powerful. What are some of the differences?

- Formal networks, from Women in Communications to the U.S. chambers of commerce, exist solely to empower you and every other member.

- When you join a business network, you are not there to do volunteer work for outside groups nor to help a community cause—not this time. You become a member of a network to advance yourself. Otherwise there's no reason to join.

- At network meetings, unlike other meetings of other organizations, you can stand up and make any announcement you wish or ask for any kind of help you need. This is the one setting where you are allowed to take care of Number One: You. It's called "vested self-interest," and it's okay in networks to be interested in yourself.

- Individual power is one of the things you gain from a strong business network—the power to tap into diverse sources of information, to have a group of people who are your boosters and to be able to find answers to questions by simply making one phone call.

•••••••••••••••• *Coach's Tip* ••••••••••••••••

If you've been trying to meet some power brokers professionally but haven't been able to get through, invite
them to speak at a network meeting. They won't say no to
a group. And you'll get to spend invaluable time with them.

••

Men have a head start when it comes to networking. The old
boys network probably was born on the golf course, where men
make so many big-money deals that it's no wonder it's called
"the greens." Though the smoke in "smoke-filled" rooms, hopefully, has been outlawed, men still almost naturally get together
to talk things over and give one another support—whether or
not they actually like each other. And the camaraderie probably
started back in Little League days, which is why women fought
so hard to open up Little League to girls as well as boys.

•••••••••••••••• *Coach's Tip* ••••••••••••••••

Networks are another form of teamwork. Women also
need to join a team.

••

Employed women for decades have been left out of the
process called networking. While young boys were encouraged
to be on sports teams, to learn to give tips to individuals that will
help the whole group achieve success and to argue passionately
but not go away mad—young girls were isolated into individual
activities such as playing with dolls and told not to argue.

When the second wave of the women's movement hit the
United States in the 1970s, women began to worry about how so
many young girls were socialized into not trusting one another
and not working together. When consciousness raising in the
late 1970s brought to light the many inequities women shared,
especially employed women, an answer to the old boys network
emerged: women's networks.

I was covering women's employment issues way back then, as
I am now, and even I was astounded at the way women in busi-

ness, professions and the trades all over the country—from St. Michaels, Maryland, to Yakima, Washington—began organizing and joining networks. Women's networks proliferated everywhere and expanded from employment issues to include support networks, health and sports, political and labor, and artistic networks.

•••••••••••••••• *Coach's Tip* ••••••••••••••••

Join a network today for the same reason women did by the thousands starting in the 1970s: Networks work.

••

When my book, *Women's Networks*, was published in 1979, I was proud that I had managed to identify—with names, addresses and phone numbers—some 1,400 women's networks. Today there are thousands of women's networks, from All the Good Old Girls to Women in Science.

The reason almost every professional association of both women and men also has its own, powerful women's group is that women, left out of decision-making roles in male-dominated groups, seek each other out and create their own network within a network. In this way they overcome some of the barriers created by male attitudes that affect the direction of the entire profession in general and opportunities for individual women in particular.

What I'm talking about is access, and I'm so enthusiastic about networking because it gives access to those who otherwise might not have it. My theory has long been that if I could only get into the men's room, where the old boys congregate, I'd probably by now be publisher of one of the biggest newspapers in the United States—which I'm not.

•••••••••••••••• *Coach's Tip* ••••••••••••••••

Even if an organization is male dominated, women also should join professional associations that have both women and men members. Men hold the doors to advancement in most fields of endeavor, so it's important to become part of their buddy system through associations.

••

But remember that not all men are privy to the latest news of company changes, who's leaving, new projects planned or salary ranges—no matter how often they go to the men's room.

·················· *Coach's Tip* ················

Women need formal networks more than men do, because men have powerful, ongoing informal networks that keep going on their own momentum. Women need networks to crash the glass ceiling, to combat rampant pay inequities and to find out what's going on. But men need networks, too.

··

"I met a guy at a cocktail party I haven't seen since college," a management instructor at a community college told me. "While we were catching up on our lives, he happened to mention that his company was thinking of introducing diversity training— which is right up my alley.

"He gave me a name and number to call, and even before a firm decision was made by the company to have training sessions to sensitize management to a multicultural workforce, I was able to get in there and pitch my services."

Because the instructor was on the inside track at an early stage of discussion, he was able to show the company how important such training is, how to implement it and who should take it. Not surprisingly, the instructor was hired as a consultant to head the company's new diversity training program.

·················· *Coach's Tip* ················

Join your high school or college alumni group, and when you pick up information by networking, act on it quickly.

··

If you personally will not benefit from the information you have learned firsthand, pass it along to another qualified member of your network. But don't give away anything you can use for yourself—that's not networking. That's self-destructive.

················· *Coach's Tip* ·················

If you recommend someone for a position you learned about through networking, make sure the person is qualified. You will be judged by the quality of those you recommend.
··

"I heard at a network meeting that one of the women in my department at work was going to resign because she wanted to go to law school full-time," said an assistant manager who is an active networker. "Though our department's small, this was the first time I'd heard about it. She hadn't said a word to any of us."

But the assistant manager knew of an administrative assistant—let's call her Jane—who was qualified and eager to move up to the next position. And the woman planning to leave held that position. "I told Jane about the possibility of the job she wanted coming open, and I urged her to do what she could to be considered for it."

With encouragement from the assistant manager, Jane summoned up all her courage and asked her colleague if what she heard was true about her going to law school. It was. Jane then asked her to help her qualify for the job. She did, and by the time the resignation was public, Jane knew how to do the work.

"Jane got the job, the company got an excellent worker to do the job, and I got a loyal coworker who would do anything in the world for me—not a bad deal," the assistant manager said.

················· *Coach's Tip* ·················

Don't abuse the confidentiality of information you acquire through networking—or you'll never get any more. But if it's not confidential, make it work for you either directly or indirectly.
··

To network effectively, it's important to know the structure of these business organizations. Your career coach already has explained the differences between informal, casual networks and highly organized, formal ones. Additionally, each of these networks can be organized in three different ways: (1) professional, (2) general and (3) in-house networks.

Let's take a close-up and personal look at each of these three networks:

1. *The professional network.* This most popular form of network is made up of people in the same career field. Their common bond is in promoting their particular line of work—and themselves. Often such groups offer certification and other credentials for members. Some are so large and powerful that they also act as lobbying groups for their constituents. Examples of professional networks and associations are the American Medical Association, American Women in Radio and Television and the National Board for Certified Counselors.

   Since most professional networks have national memberships, they also have healthy budgets that allow them to provide members with a variety of helpful publications. More importantly, most professional networks offer excellent career advice and maintain job banks.

·················· *Coach's Tip* ················

Your professional network gives you a leg up in your field. Join one, no matter what the fees are, and attend their national conventions and chapter meetings.

··

2. *The general network.* This form of networking cuts across professions, jobs and ranks. The variety of information a general network offers is invaluable. The mix of people provides many layers of data about what's happening in the business world in general and gives you contacts for whatever you need to get your job done. Among the general networks are such groups as the National Committee on Pay Equity and the Chicago Network, Inc.

   Since general networks aren't focused solely on one profession, they rarely have job banks—though by asking individual members for help, you can get a wealth of information about anything you need to know, including job opportunities. General networks often have especially interesting speakers for their meetings simply because they are not confined to one subject alone.

•••••••••••••••••• *Coach's Tip* ••••••••••••••••••

Join a professional network, and then join a general one, too.
•••

3. *The in-house network.* This form of networking is the most tricky. It's made up of employees in the same company but definitely is not a union (the word employers hate most to hear). The tricky part is first gaining the confidence and permission of your employer to create an informal business network in the first place.

In-house business networks are a natural to get the information you need to get ahead in the job you now have. Working with your colleagues to improve your skills or to get together to discuss what's happening in your department or unit, or to meet informally with senior management, is extremely beneficial. In-house networks often are formed by secretaries who want to move ahead, new mothers, employees who are working for their MBAs and by those with a special interest in computers. The feeling of knowing, on a daily basis, that people right there, where you work, are on your side and want to help you is one that *really* can make your day!

•••••••••••••••••• *Coach's Tip* ••••••••••••••••••

If your company has an in-house network, join it if it meets your needs. It could turn out to be your most important business connection.
•••

Belonging to an in-house business network can accelerate your career advancement in the firm, but first make sure that the in-house network has the complete sanction and support of the company. The point of an in-house network is to succeed in your present job at your present company. If the network is suspect because management fears it is a prelude to union activity or rebellion in the ranks, the network will be ineffective and your career there will come to a grinding halt.

"A group of us across the company were chosen to serve on a corporate task force to improve productivity," a manufacturing engineer for a large corporation told me. "The ten members, all Young Turks, including me, had been carefully selected by our managers—we were clearly on the rise, and each was so sharp! The strange part is that most of us had never heard of the others.

"We met weekly for one year, worked very hard to come up with good ideas and got to know and respect one another. We also learned an awful lot about what was going on in the rest of the company, the problems and the future direction. After the project was done, we found we missed each other and wanted to get together."

The task force members decided to make their group an ongoing one, albeit informal. Even though they decided not to meet on company time as they had done previously but to have lunch together at least once a month, they did something very smart.

"We went to the executive who had organized the original task force and told her we planned to get together informally," the engineer said. "We wanted to make sure the company knew we were continuing as a group—and that our sole interest was advancing the good of the company. She thought it was a great idea and asked if she could join us from time to time."

Two years later every single member of the original task force has been promoted, and each is up to the minute on what's happening throughout the company. And the Young Turks still meet.

· · · · · · · · · · · · · · · · *Coach's Tip* · · · · · · · · · · · · · · · ·

If you can't find a network that meets your professional or work needs, form one of your own and name yourself Queen or King.

· ·

Here are some questions to consider when setting up your own network:

- *Should your network be small or large?* Let the content determine the form. In any case, you'll probably want to start out small.

- *Should the network be centered around one profession or many?* Since you're the one doing the hard work of organizing the network, make it be whichever best serves your own personal purposes.

- *How do you select members?* Because business networks have thousands of potential members, once again the ground rules will be up to you simply as a form of crowd control. People will want to join an energetic network of those who have something to offer others and who also want to move ahead. Start by inviting five of your most trusted colleagues to join and brainstorm membership rules with them. Don't be elitist or discriminate against anyone. The point is to get as many qualified people in, not to keep people out—whether or not you personally like them.

- *How do you recruit members?* Get your core group of five to ask ten people each, and see where it goes from there. Compile a mailing list of at least 25 people before taking the next step. However, for informal or in-house networks, having a solid base of five members is sufficient to get started.

- *How important are meetings?* Most networkers network every day in person, by telephone, fax, letters or whatever is available. Nonetheless, monthly meetings are essential to make networking work. And having speakers who are prominent in their fields and at the cutting edge of change is a sure way to make sure that attendance is high. It's also a way of gaining access to important people you want to meet but have no other way of doing so.

- *Who actually runs the network?* You do, at first, with the help of a board of directors you select. Still, it's up to you to make the decisions about dues, bylaws, incorporation, meeting places, newsletters, directories, mailings, etc. Founders of networks wear the Boss hat, but if you're smart (and you have to be smart to start a network), you'll step down after a year and let the membership pick a new leader—which they will.

"I helped start a network of people in my city in my profession," a businesswoman told me. "I needed to surround myself with people in my field, since I was the only one who did the job at my office."

No associations existed in her field, so her network caught on quickly, she says. As president, she personally got to know all the movers and shakers in her area of expertise, a lot about their companies and many of their contacts.

"My network is two years old and growing," she said. "I'm invited to give talks all over the city and often am interviewed by the media about questions pertaining to my field. I've earned a new respect at work, too—they didn't even know I existed before or that what I do is so important." She added, "I love networking. It really works!"

· · · · · · · · · · · · · · · · · *Coach's Tip* · · · · · · · · · · · · · · · ·

When it comes to business networks, don't leave home without one.

· ·

14

Your Own
Continuing
Education Program

Since the late 1980s, the United States, like the rest of the world, has been a service-producing economy. Ninety percent of the jobs created in the 1990s and well into the 21st century will require *thinking* abilities—not *making* abilities. Translated, that means brains not brawn are what will get you the job you want and help you keep it.

In a high-tech society, if you are illiterate, you simply won't survive economically. There will be a proliferation of the Haves and Have-nots in the world of work: The Haves will be those who are well educated and have ongoing upgradings of their skills and professional requirements. The Have-nots will be those who are poorly educated and will not have upgraded skills.

Coach's Tip

Be a Have, not a Have-not. Get all the education and training you can.

Another fact of work life is that you must be computer literate to stay in the game. You'll frequently have to update your computer skills to keep on the cutting edge of change—and to keep your job.

·················· *Coach's Tip* ··················

To *qualify* for a job, you must have credentials beyond high school, either vocational or technical training or a college degree. A high school diploma no longer suffices for a good-paying job with a future. To *keep* your job, the same credentials are needed: something beyond high school. The more, the merrier for you, especially in your paycheck.

··

The service-producing sector needs workers with specialized skills, people who are computer literate, intelligent, good communicators, team players and, because of the international marketplace, able to speak more than one language and to understand and respect other cultures.

By the year 2000, the U.S. Department of Labor estimates that three out of every four workers currently employed will need retraining for the new jobs of the next century. If you are the average worker of the next century, you will change professions three times over your work life and jobs six times—often because of the new technology, which will make your job obsolete or radically reconstructed. You will have to be your own smart machine.

In view of these projections, the importance of continuing your education over the lifetime of your career becomes an obvious training exercise to be performed daily, a necessary muscle toner for success.

·················· *Coach's Tip* ··················

Enroll in as many courses as you can handle, ones that will give momentum to your professional advancement.

··

Learn a new language, study humanities, take a math course, learn a new computer program, study business or technical writing, enroll in a management course. And then take a course you simply enjoy, learning solely for the joy of learning, to expand your mind and to think new thoughts. Or, as I like to say, "blow your brain."

You have several ways to increase your intellectual capabilities, and, if you can, try to be involved in each of them:

- Buy or borrow books or videos on subjects that interest you, and study on your own time, at your own pace.

- Sign up for individual adult high school, community college or college courses that are important to round out your education. Pay for them yourself.

- Take a variety of individual courses or lectures, not necessarily leading to a specific degree, and ask your employer to reimburse you under the federal education reimbursement plan that allows employers to deduct—and reimburse to you—a portion of your expenses.

- Enroll in a degree program, at undergraduate or graduate level. Decide if it's better for you to pay for your studies yourself. If you pay, it means that no strings are attached, and you will be able to leave the company, if you want to, when you complete the degree. (In most cases if the company pays, it will ask you to promise verbally or to sign a contract to stay on for from three to five years.) If you want the company to pay, either because you can't afford to do so or you want the company to have a vested interest in your acquiring new skills and promotions, apply for reimbursement.

- Accept every invitation the company offers you to enroll in its own training programs or to attend outside workshops, lectures and conferences. You will not only learn important skills but will make important contacts within and outside the company.

- If you're not invited to participate, don't be shy about asking permission to be part of helpful in-house workshops and training programs and to attend outside lectures and conferences that interest you. If you always wait to be asked, you may not get the chance to learn more. The best scenario for you to enroll in outside training sessions is for the company to pay for them. If it won't pay, ask permission to attend on company time. If you can't get permission for that either, go anyway on your own time, and pay for it yourself. It's worth it.

·················· *Coach's Tip* ··················

T ry to get the best grades in any course or program you sign up for, and don't miss any classes—even if you miss work that day!

··

After all, you're an adult, and you want to get the most out of the time you have to put in to learn something new. And since most companies will not reimburse you if you don't have a certain grade point average (which they determine), you want to get good grades to pass their scrutiny, to show them how smart you are, how promotable you are—and to be reimbursed.

·················· *Coach's Tip* ··················

A sking for further education and training is not like asking for a raise: keeping you current is something companies actively *want* to do. So ask for what you want, as often as you want to, and keep asking until you get it.

··

A political science major from Duke University got a job with a firm that provides litigation services. Her starting salary was $35,000 a year—not a bad salary, at that. At the firm, she became interested in marketing but quickly realized that since it wasn't the main business of her company, she had limited opportunities in their employ. Because she had some on-the-job experience, she reasoned that if she applied elsewhere for a marketing job, she'd surely get one. But she couldn't.

She finally realized that what she needed was more education, and in particular, an MBA—because that's what companies with major marketing departments look for. She quit her job, got her MBA from Dartmouth College within a year and had a job as a marketing trainee even before she was graduated. Her starting salary: $60,000 a year plus a hiring bonus.

·················· *Coach's Tip* ················

If you know exactly what degree or what skill you must have to get a job or to take your next step upward and have some savings or unemployment compensation to live on, consider taking a leave of absence or even quitting your present job to go to school full-time. It may pay off for you in the long run.

Studying full-time may be a necessity, especially if your current skills are obsolete. A student enrolled at Elgin Community College in Elgin, Illinois, was laid off from his job of 25 years as an electronic maintenance technician. Sad to say, he unsuccessfully looked for another job for almost a year. He had quit school after the eighth grade and realized that his education and skills needed upgrading. His first step was to get his high school diploma—a really smart move.

It had been 41 years since he had been in school, but still unemployed, he next enrolled at Elgin to work toward an associate degree in industrial maintenance and certification in heating and air-conditioning. Armed with relevant new skills, he found a job as a maintenance mechanic and continued attending night classes at the community college to complete his degree. "Now that I've broken the ice," he says, "I'll probably go on taking courses for the rest of my life."

··············· *Coach's Tip* ················

If you take courses for the rest of your life, you will be set for the rest of your life.

The new focus on training and development—an old story in Europe, where apprenticeship programs begin at the high school level and lead to high-skill, high-wage jobs—was precipitated by educators who long ago realized that they were turning out high school and college graduates unprepared to do the vital jobs being created by the Information Age.

But just as serious attention to the matter came from the people who have the money to do something about the lack of critical skills among U.S. workers: employers whose bottom lines are seriously affected by an unskilled, illiterate workforce and who also recognize the financial necessity of improving the abilities of the best and the brightest in their employ. International corporate giants such as Motorola, Inc., on the cutting edge of change in semiconductors and electronics, and Arthur Andersen & Co., the prestigious accounting and consulting firm, are among the industry leaders who actually have set up their own teaching establishments for employees.

Motorola's is called Motorola University and has a vast curriculum of programs for employees at every level. Motorola's commitment to continuing education is so strong that employees are required to take at least 40 hours of additional education every year either at Motorola University or in outside classes— most of it on company time and at company expense.

Arthur Andersen has purchased a former college, with classrooms, dormitories, convocation center, swimming pool, tennis court and running track. Most of the company's training is done at the campus, and the attractive setting is another incentive for employees to participate.

The rush to education is so rapidly accelerating that educational institutions are opening adult education classes where students are most likely to go: shopping malls. According to *The New York Times*, one such school, Mall of America, has classes held right in the megamall in Bloomington, Minnesota. Its vital presence means that not only can you shop till you drop, you also can learn till you drop. It offers classes both to its staff and the public in a variety of subjects ranging from high school equivalency diplomas to mall management, retailing and graduate courses. The unit is under the direction of the University of St. Thomas in St. Paul.

Spreading the word that valuing workplace education should be a lifelong commitment for employers and employees alike is the goal of Harry E. Featherstone, known as "the CEO with a mission." As reported in the *Chicago Tribune*, Featherstone, head of Will-Burt Company in Orrville, Ohio, travels the nation speaking to businesses, workers and educational groups. Featherstone shares his compelling message of commitment to workplace education: "Any company of any size that is not into education by the year 2000 will either be owned by someone else or working strictly locally."

Featherstone practices what he preaches. Since 1985, when he introduced a companywide program, his workers have participated in courses in blueprint reading, human relations, self-esteem, integrity, leadership, curiosity, discipline, creativity, spatial thinking and openness. The only courses I would add to his curriculum are assertiveness training for the men and aggressiveness training for the women, also both essential in the new world of work.

A commitment to workplace education has to come from the top, and slowly the message of its importance is permeating U.S. business and industry. And just as slowly, workers are also beginning to realize the urgent need to keep up their skills and add new ones—often, just to stay in place.

·················· *Coach's Tip* ··················

If you want to stay in the running, continue your education. And then, continue it some more.

··

When I urge you never to stop exercising your brain power over your whole work life, I realize I'm talking to adults, mostly employed adults, who probably haven't been in school for years and who celebrated wildly for several days when they got their last degree or finished their last course. Nonetheless, the number of older students enrolled in colleges and technical schools is on the rise. In fact, the average age of a community college student is close to 30 years.

"This continuing trend [of older students] is rooted in the changing economy and rapid technological advances that require continuous, updated training," according to Dr. Drew Allbritten, executive director of the American Association of Adult and Continuing Education, quoted in *ReCareering Newsletter*.

·················· *Coach's Tip* ··················

Don't let age or how long you've been out of school and away from the world of education keep you from advancing your career by degrees.

··

I know personally how hard it is to hold down a full-time job and take a course, even just one night a week. Early in my career of working for newspapers, I signed up for a course in short story writing to broaden potential outlets for my writing. I confess up front that I thought the course would be a breeze: I had already written six stories, which I planned to use to meet classroom assignments, and I had read the books and collections required for the course. My vision of "continuing education" was merely to show up at the classes and absorb what I could from the professor and classmates and use them as a critical sounding board and cheering squad for my writing.

But it didn't work out that way. First of all, I was exhausted before, during and after each class. I had expected that. But what I hadn't anticipated was being exhilarated, excited and turned on by the subject matter. I quickly realized it wasn't going to be a breeze; I'd have to be serious and do some real work.

I put aside my "canned" short stories, wrote all new ones and spent more time than I had planned preparing for the course. I learned more than I had planned, too. I knew by the end of the course that my short stories were passable—I even sold some of them to magazines—but short story writing, I learned, is not what I do best. I had been right to choose journalism as my main source of income. However, I still write short stories just for myself and network with the people I met in that class.

I was fortunate to have learned long ago the seriousness of continuing education and since then have a much more mature approach to expanding my mind. When I sign up for classes, I make sure that I have the time to do them right. This self-knowledge led me to delay studying for a doctorate because I realized that I simply would not be able to do it and hold down my very-full-time jobs both at work and at home. But it still is my dream for the future. In addition to the education I would get, I also like the idea of having the title "Dr." before my name: it doesn't indicate marital status or gender and suggests great wealth!

·················· *Coach's Tip* ················

When you take a course or attend a workshop, be open to everything going on. You may be surprised about what you learn about yourself, as well as the subject, and how you grow.

··

Adults with full-time, demanding jobs, families at home and other responsibilities are among those flooding classrooms, both part-time and full-time, day and night. Survival is the key to balancing so many obligations, because it clearly would be most unfortunate to expend so much effort for so many years to qualify for something you want to do—and then to be too burnt out ever to do it.

Here's some advice to ease the pain of reentry into academic settings for courses not provided in-house at your place of employment:

- Decide what you want to do and what it will take to get you there. Talk things over with a high school, college or private career counselor.

- Figure out the best way to achieve your goal. Do you want to take one course at a time and see if you are on the right track, or go full-time immediately to get there as quickly as possible? Factor into the equation how your new studies will impact on your life, your job and your family.

- Shop around for the course you want at the institution that's right for you. Also check to see if the school has a career counseling and placement center. Its services are free to you as a student, and you will need all the support and direction you can get. If it's geographically convenient to your home or worksite, so much the better.

- Get credit for life experience. When you list your credentials, include the fact that you've done volunteer work for years, that you ran a scout troop or did a newsletter for a community group, taught literacy classes at the library, arranged tours, lived in another country and are fluent in its language. Some colleges that are eager to attract mature students give credit, where appropriate, for experiences and knowledge acquired outside formal academic institutions.

- Give yourself frequent reality checks. Am I actually learning what I need to know? Am I enjoying this? Am I taking too heavy of a load? Am I in the right setting?

- Use weekends and vacation time to do the heavy-duty work of writing papers and taking tests instead of squeezing them into your workweek.

- Form a study group with your classmates for support, for people to do your homework with and who will give you the information you need when you have to miss classes.

- Give yourself a deserved rest at the end of each term to reenergize yourself. Besides, you deserve it.

· · · · · · · · · · · · · · · · *Coach's Tip* · · · · · · · · · · · · · · · ·

Make sure that your supervisor knows you are taking courses, even if the firm doesn't reimburse you, and even if you feel it has nothing to do with your current job, such as a word processor studying robotics. Believe me, it matters.
· ·

Employers will recognize your ambition and work ethic, no matter what you're studying. As one human resources executive says, "Employers don't give promotions just because an employee gets a degree or completes a needed course, but it does demonstrate your commitment to education and your profession. And somewhere down the road, you will be rewarded for your effort with a chance to move ahead."

Or learn from Aristotle, the Greek philosopher, who said more than 2,000 years ago, "Education is the best provision for old age."

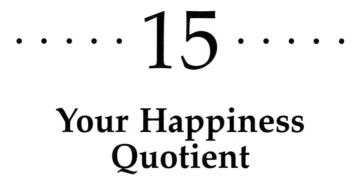

15

Your Happiness Quotient

Few things complicate your life more than spending eight to ten hours a day, five to six days a week, at a job you don't like, doing something you don't want to do.
— Elaine St. James, *Simplify Your Life*

Author Elaine St. James is talking about happiness, one of my favorite subjects. It is not an oxymoron to talk about being happy on the job. In fact, it is almost a necessity because you spend so much of your life at work, and if you are unhappy there, you are *very* unhappy.

· · · · · · · · · · · · · · · · *Coach's Tip* · · · · · · · · · · · · · · · ·

Try to select a job, workplace and colleagues that make you happy, even if it costs you something in salary.

· ·

One of my favorite people at work is my colleague at the *Chicago Tribune*, veteran journalist Larry Townsend. What I like best about him—in addition to the fact that he is one of the few people who plays tennis with me without openly sobbing—is that each day Larry greets me and his other coworkers in this manner: "Happiness!" he says with a broad smile.

That one phrase, which I think is far more inclusive and has far more substance than the incredibly trite "Have a good day," raises the issue quite early in the morning that working and contentment might possibly go hand in hand. "I just want to get people thinking about it," Larry explained—happily. And I know firsthand that he does, because his cheery greeting sets the tone for *my* day.

· · · · · · · · · · · · · · · · *Coach's Tip* · · · · · · · · · · · · · · · ·

Here's another reason to try to be reasonably happy at work: Unhappiness can make you sick.

· ·

Stresses such as conflict at work can make people more vulnerable to infectious disease, according to Dr. Arthur Stone, a psychologist at the medical school of the State University of New York at Stony Brook. According to *The New York Times,* Stone's research shows that happiness has a far more lasting effect on your health than unhappiness: "The small boost to the immune system offered by a pleasant event can persist as long as two days, while the negative effects of a stressful encounter mainly take their toll on one day." And that can feel like a very long 24 hours.

The immune system takes the hardest hit, the study shows, from work problems, criticism from the boss, frustrating or irritating encounters with colleagues at work, the pressure of deadlines and a heavy workload.

· · · · · · · · · · · · · · · · *Coach's Tip* · · · · · · · · · · · · · · · ·

Nobody is suggesting that you must be happy every moment at work. But if your work arrangements really get you, do something about them—at least whatever is in your power to change.

· ·

Although most career consultants deplore anyone's spending a few moments looking out the window, your career coach is for it 100 percent—if you're lucky enough to work anywhere in the vicinity of a window. Believe it or not, studies show that what we've often demeaned as "windowgazing" actually is good for the mind. A natural view refreshes you mentally and clears out the cobwebs of discontent that may have accumulated.

"Having a window is important to people," says Rachel Kaplan, a University of Michigan professor of psychology and natural resources in an interview with *Knight-Ridder/Tribune*. And Kaplan is not just talking about the high status that having a window confers on the employee who has it. "More than that," she says, "it's what they can see out of the window that influences satisfaction with their job and perception of their job performance."

In a study of 600 workers, Kaplan found that those with window views of nature were "significantly" more enthusiastic about their jobs and less frustrated. In other words, they were happier. On the other hand, workers without windows were more likely to suffer "attention fatigue," be more easily distracted and more irritable. In other words, they were unhappy.

· · · · · · · · · · · · · · · · *Coach's Tip* · · · · · · · · · · · · · · · ·

You deserve a break today, and if you don't have access to a window, take a brief "recess," go outside and commune with nature—even if your office is on a busy, congested, downtown street.

· ·

Workers try to create their own happiness in a variety of ways, despite daunting odds. Many say the best way to relieve tension—and the absence of feeling tense often means feeling happy—is to exercise daily, to swim, work out, ride a bike, walk vigorously and whatever else makes you and your body happy.

My friends who play volleyball, tennis, racquetball or basketball—which makes them very happy all day long—do so early in the morning. "I'd rather be tired for work than for tennis," is how I myself feel about it.

················ *Coach's Tip* ················

Work as hard at finding time for exercise to relieve stress and for the sheer pleasure in it as you do to arrange lunches with friends. In fact, lunchtime also is a good time to take a long walk and smell the roses—even if there are no roses.

··

The Declaration of Independence promises us that in the United States we have the right to the pursuit of happiness. It's a nice thought, but the implication is that the closest we ever can get to actual happiness is in the pursuit of it. Well, I want more for you. I want the real thing: I prefer not only to pursue happiness but to achieve it. Especially at work.

················ *Coach's Tip* ················

Figure out what makes you happy on the job, and pay attention to the results.

··

In my book, *The 100 Best Jobs for the 1990s & Beyond*, I included a list of questions I call "reality check." Unlike the questions I list in Chapter 1 to help determine which is the right job for you, these queries emphasize matters that may not be completely essential but which have the power to make you happy or unhappy.

As your career coach, I have given much thought to what questions you should ask yourself about your happiness quotient. And I keep coming up with the same questions I presented in my previous book, questions that seemed to touch a nerve and were widely reprinted nationally. Thus, the following ten questions seem to me the right questions to ask again:

1. Do you look forward to going to work each day?

2. At the end of the day, do you feel a sense of accomplishment?

3. Do you respect your employers, their goals, ethics and professional expertise?

4. Are you doing what you do best, using the skills and knowledge you have acquired for the profession of your choice?

5. Do you feel you're being paid fairly, including salary, benefits and other perks?

6. Are you positioned to move ahead in the next two or three years?

7. Does your company have a commitment to continuing education and training to keep you up-to-date in your field and in the new technology?

8. Does your employer know your professional goals and discuss with you on a regular basis the skills you need to move into the next job level?

9. Is your present employer concerned about issues such as flexible hours, parental leave, job sharing, child and elder care and wellness programs?

10. Are you satisfied with the balance between your time commitment to your personal goals/responsibilities and your professional goals/responsibilities?

There are no correct answers to these questions, of course, but they can serve as a guidepost to your own personal quest for happiness and keep you in touch with what matters to you and what does not.

················ *Coach's Tip* ················

Test your happiness quotient at least once a year—especially around the time of your performance review.
··

Even when the unemployment picture remains unsettled, with jobs being created and lost at the same firms, employees often call to say that they are extremely unhappy in their jobs but don't want to leave the town or city they work in. They assume that only one location in the world will make them happy, which, in the global marketplace that is now a fact of life, might lead, if not to unhappiness, possibly to unemployment.

"I was offered an excellent job in computer programming in Colorado, a really good job, but I didn't want to leave Boston," said a reader who lost his job in the hard times that befell the high-technology industry in New England in the recession of the late 1980s. "I'd been unemployed for two years, though, and I was worried. It was too good an opportunity to pass up."

He said he delayed as long as he could and finally, quite unhappily, made the move. Two years later he reports he couldn't be happier. "I know it sounds superficial, especially for a computer nerd, but in contemplating the move I forgot about all the good skiing out here. That's a real plus that no one ever mentioned."

·················· *Coach's Tip* ··················

It's okay to take a job because the location—not the job—offers you something that makes you very happy, such as a chance to surf or water-ski, to be involved in arts and crafts or to be near your favorite zoo or sports team. Or simply because you prefer warm weather to cold, or vice versa.

··

One of the factors that cuts into personal happiness with deep flesh wounds is a rigid workplace, which results in a rigid work-week, rigid workday and rigid workers. And uptight workers are not happy campers.

Because everyone works such long hours, personal time spent with family, friends and doing things for yourself becomes more important than ever. The need for downtime used to be described as a "quality of life" issue, a term that went out of style when downsizing and restructuring began proliferating. But the universal need for time of one's own, like a room of one's own, has not diminished.

·················· *Coach's Tip* ··················

If you want flextime, job sharing, compressed work-week, permanent part-time work or to be a telecommuter (work from home), you will have to be the one to make the request to do so and, in most cases, devise a plan.

··

Unless you are among the minority of workers who have a contract and flexible work hours and family issues are part of your contract, or unless you are fortunate enough to be employed by a forward-looking company that has in place the helpful policies you need and want to restore balance to your life, it's up to you to redesign your job. According to Maria Laqueur and Donna Dickinson, authors of *Breaking Out of 9 to 5: How To Redesign Your Job To Fit You,* employees are "lobbying in ever-increasing numbers to create new work arrangements for themselves. A virtual workplace revolution is in the offing. . . ."

Here are your coach's suggestions for creating a flexible schedule for yourself:

- Focus on the one option that appeals to you most. In other words, ask for one thing you want at a time.

- Research your company's policies about flexible schedules.

- Talk to others who have work arrangements similar to the one you want.

- Determine how the work will get done with the proposed new schedule.

- If your plan is accepted, make yourself indispensable and be visible to ensure job security and career advancement.

·················· *Coach's Tip* ··················

Don't give up if your plan for flexibility is rejected the first time around. Keep bringing up the subject in a non-confrontational way. Eventually you may succeed.

··

I've had a lot of unusual and surprising inquiries in my years as a career coach, but the one that gives me the most pause is a letter from a woman who recently got a new job at a large corporation—the job of her dreams, she said—and got married shortly thereafter. "It would make my husband and me so happy to have a family," she wrote. "I can hardly wait to have a baby. But I'm worried about jeopardizing my career. Do you think it would be a good idea for me to discuss this matter with my boss, to make sure it's okay to go ahead?"

I understood her concern about not hurting her advancement in a job she so highly prizes, but I emphasized to her that she and her husband alone have to make the decision to have a family—without any input from her manager. I assured her that the federal Pregnancy Discrimination Act prevents her from being fired when she becomes pregnant and the federal Family and Medical Leave Act protects her job after the baby is born.

· · · · · · · · · · · · · · · · *Coach's Tip* · · · · · · · · · · · · · · · · ·

Don't consult your boss if you are thinking about having a baby. It's nobody's business but your own, and it's illegal for your employer to discuss the matter with you.

· ·

On the other hand—and at the same time—I also received a letter from a very happy woman who had left her job two years earlier after the birth of her baby and before the Family and Medical Leave Act went into effect. She lost her previous job and was now looking for work. Fortunately for her, her husband earned enough money to keep the family going during her absence as a wage earner and also had full benefits. What delighted me about this job seeker is that on her resume, she filled in the previous two years of her work experience in this way: "Adorable baby."

Just as having a family makes some workers happy and not having a family makes others just as happy, you may be surprised to learn, as I was, about some of the work factors that may be involved in your happiness quotient.

Most research shows that strong leadership skills among top management make employees most happy—proving to some receptive employers that money isn't everything. But a recent study of 150 human resources managers by Office Team, a national staffing firm based in Menlo Park, California, has a different finding: Forty-seven percent said that praise and recognition is what makes their employees happy. Also high on the happiness scale were promotions, job security, work environment and compensation and benefits.

•••••••••••••••••••• *Coach's Tip* ••••••••••••••••••

Employers must be concerned about their employees' happiness, if not from a humanistic point of view, then because job satisfaction leads to high morale and increased productivity.

•••

I'm sure the job satisfaction surveys are accurate because they make so much sense, but one aspect to happiness in a work environment keeps getting passed over as one of the questions that should be asked: Do you have control over your work?

Most people don't have control over their work unless they're the owners, but studies comparing managers to low-level employees show that control of at least some aspects of their jobs makes the managers much happier people than those who merely take orders. I stressed in Chapter 11 that taking charge of your career is the only way to ensure success. It's also the only way to ensure happiness.

•••••••••••••••••••• *Coach's Tip* ••••••••••••••••••

When you analyze your career and how it's going, factor in how happy you are with your job and your life— they overlap.

•••

Ask yourself if your career plans and dreams include goals that make you happy. Are you paying enough attention to what makes you happy in your personal life as well—or is personal happiness just something you squeeze into the time left over from work?

The new executive of a group of community mental health centers told *The New York Times* how excited he was to be part of a growing company. The security of a full-time job meant a lot to him, too, because he had been a self-employed consultant for five years. But the executive did have a complaint. "I never get to see my son's karate class now," he said.

People who have been away from a structured workplace often are relieved to be back again in the traditional 9 to 5 mode, but the change in lifestyle can be overwhelming and requires a great deal of adjustment. "I was out of the workplace for ten years, raising my family, running my household and occasionally working part-time as a marketing consultant—from home," a reader told me. "Now I'm back in an office full-time, and it's so hard to get used to not being my own boss. But I have no choice."

She was so unhappy about the situation, she says, that at one point she considered quitting. "But we need the money, or I wouldn't be here in the first place," she said. "So I worked out a compromise."

Her "compromise" was to clear with her manager exactly what is expected of her each week and to deliver the work with top-notch professionalism—but at her own pace and often, at her choice of location. Because she is a highly valued professional, she is permitted to work 14 hours one day and only five the next and to move between her office and home as she wishes. She always is up-to-date in her work.

· · · · · · · · · · · · · · · · *Coach's Tip* · · · · · · · · · · · · · · · ·

Ask for what you want. You might get it. If not, make it happen. And show your gratitude by being a top performer.
· ·

A secretary for a large computer firm was unhappy about constantly being passed over for promotion. "Because I was a secretary, I wasn't even considered for any job, not even the lowest entry-level management job," said the secretary, who has a bachelor's degree and an MBA. "I took a secretarial job because it was the only opening at the company at the time and I liked the company. But I had locked myself into a dead-end job."

After repeatedly being passed over and complaining about it vigorously, the secretary realized that she couldn't fight the sexist stigma of being an administrative assistant. And thinking about it, she realized that the company she had thought was so wonderful really wasn't. "Based on all of this, I decided to leave the company," she said. "I plan to get my own business going and probably make more money. And I'll be able to spend more time with my family, away from the stress of the workplace."

She is quite happy now and was smart enough to leave her job without any recriminations or accusations. Not everyone does that. When some people are unhappy, they make sure that everyone around them at work and at home shares in it.

················· *Coach's Tip* ················

When someone else gets the promotion or assignment you want, don't throw a fit, clean out your desk, bang on empty lockers or bad-mouth the winner. It's unprofessional and counterproductive for the future of your career.

··

While it's okay to sulk over your disappointment for a day or two—no one ever promised you happiness *every* day—don't carry on for too long. You'll lose everyone's sympathy, if you had it in the first place, very quickly. After some public mourning, go back to being your cheerful, professional self—or start hunting for a job that makes you much happier. It's not up to your employer to make up for your disappointment.

I strongly caution you to keep your cool amid the madness of the workplace for another reason: Venting your unhappiness by screaming or yelling and having fits, despite feeling so good, is harmful to your health. Doesn't that make you angry?

Despite my warning not to lose your cool during work hours, one way to deal with unhappiness is essential, to my way of thinking: crying.

················ *Coach's Tip* ················

R̲ead this and weep: Crying is a normal way to show frustration. So don't be afraid to cry, even in the office.
··

"Tears in the workplace are considered weak because men have been taught not to cry," said Jeanne M. Plous, a psychologist who has published a study called "Tears and Weeping Among Professional Women: In Search of New Understanding." Plous stresses that when you are stressed out, tears are "the body's way of regulating the flow of energy and emotion. If we don't cry, we weaken our systems."

Men, too, can benefit from crying, instead of getting angry. I personally advise crying every day as a wonderful release. To assure personal happiness, I further advise that you start each day by saying out loud, "It's not my fault!" Say it loudly and don't forget it, even when things are rough and even when it may be your fault in some part.

················ *Coach's Tip* ················

B̲e in touch with your professional goals, your dreams and your emotional needs. It's the stuff happiness is made of. And you deserve to be happy!
··

There's nothing metaphysical about your happiness quotient. You have to work hard to achieve it, just as you have to work hard to find the right job and keep it. The really happy news is that not only can you be happily employed yourself, you can spread that happiness by helping others along the way, as you will learn in the next chapter.

PART FOUR

Helping Others along the Way— And Yourself

16

How and Why
To Help

Many people are hesitant to help other colleagues at work because of an old, familiar fear that's summed up in the expression "No good deed goes unpunished."

Helping others get a leg up in business or industry was dealt a heavy blow long ago by the movie *All About Eve* and again more recently by *Working Girl*. The message in both movies is that the minute your back is turned or your leg broken, even trusted co-workers, possibly someone you helped advance, will do whatever they can to do you in and get your job.

That's not a pretty picture. The fact is that in the real world, in most cases, when you look out for others—at the same time that you look out for yourself—the payoff for you can be enormous. It's called doing well by doing good.

· · · · · · · · · · · · · · · · *Coach's Tip* · · · · · · · · · · · · · · · ·

Even though, as a decent human being, you should *want* to help your colleagues get good assignments and promotions, if the moral imperative to be helpful doesn't motivate you, act out of your own vested self-interest.

• •

"I was offered a special assignment that involved going out of town for several weeks," an administrative assistant told me. "I was thrilled to be considered for it, but it was just the wrong time for me to be away because my teenage kids would be out of school for spring vacation, and I knew I had to be around."

She reluctantly turned it down but mentioned the assignment to a colleague of hers, a slightly higher-ranking manager. The manager applied for the assignment before anyone else even knew the opportunity was available.

"He got the assignment, and when he came back he was put in charge of the project," the administrative assistant said. "His first act was to bring me in as second in command, and since then he always has been especially considerate of me and my family responsibilities. We work together as equals because he knows he may not have had the excellent opportunity he got if I hadn't told him about it."

The experience of this administrative assistant—who has been promoted into management—shows how by helping others, you can also help yourself.

• • • • • • • • • • • • • • • • *Coach's Tip* • • • • • • • • • • • • • • • •

Help someone at any level do better, and you will have a loyal colleague who in turn will be looking out for you.

• •

The kind of effort I'm talking about here goes even beyond networking, which to me is a very high calling. Although networking involves advancing yourself and your interests, helping others on the job is far more altruistic. It involves having a commitment to making sure that qualified, talented and deserving people have a chance to get ahead.

Reciprocity is the key to helping others, because most people know that even if they can't do anything for you right now, they'll never forget they owe you one.

Now that we've discussed how virtuous helping others is, being helpful can also stem from trying to correct a wrong. In other words, from trying to get even. Some people call that "revenge," which has ugly connotations, but trying to right a wrong can be a cleansing experience and can also help others. It certainly was a good moment for everyone when Stuart Alan Rado, nationally known consumer advocate (see Chapter 2), decided to get the goods on a dishonest career marketing firm to help others avoid his unhappy experience. At the same time, he avenged his being bilked out of thousands of dollars by an unscrupulous company that promised a job paying up to $250,000 annually—but didn't deliver.

Rado, who sought to get his money back, fought for years by researching information about career marketing firms and enlisting the aid of state authorities. He finally managed to put the offending firm and its branches out of business.

"Don't get mad; get even," said Rado. But he does much more. His own personal experience made him an expert on career scams by leading him to awareness and in-depth information about these dishonest firms. In fact, it is Rado who created the rule of thumb that when a career firm promises to get you a job by giving you "access to the hidden job market," that's the time to take your money and run.

Today Rado is a highly respected, full-time consumer advocate; has put many dishonest firms out of business; and has saved many innocent job seekers from the heartache of what he went through. Out of his desire "not to take it lying down," Rado has established an important slot for himself among the nation's job seekers and has a full-time profession that he passionately pursues in order to help others.

Here's a letter I received recently from a job seeker who had written me inquiring about the credentials of a national career firm that promised him a job if he signed a contract to pay them $2,600 in advance:

Thanks so much for your advice. I especially want to thank you for telling me about consumer advocate Rado and for giving me his phone number. I called him concerning [name of the firm deleted to protect the guilty] and learned of its troubles with the attorney generals of various states for not living up to their promises.

That phone call saved me $2,600. Thanks again!

Rado's "revenge" took him years to achieve, but most of us don't have to wait that long or work that hard to help others, directly or indirectly. Managers, in particular, are well positioned to help others almost effortlessly, because they know what's going on inside the company and are *supposed* to help others be more productive and move ahead. That's their job, and for many executives, helping their staff succeed is one of the most gratifying parts of their daily assignment.

"I have an excellent assistant, and for the past two years I've focused on teaching her and telling her everything I know about my job," a department head told me. "She's learned, and she's good. Now it's time for me to move on; I'm not needed anymore. In other words, I've achieved my goal as a manager."

I asked him how it felt not to be "needed" anymore. "It feels good to know I've really helped someone," he told me. "I'm proud of what I've achieved here and, just as good, so is the company."

················ *Coach's Tip* ················

By helping a subordinate work better or move ahead, managers also can turn dissatisfied but talented employees into allies who will always be there to help them.

··

"With a subversive subordinate who hungers for your job ... acknowledge it," writes Joan E. Rigdon in *The Wall Street Journal*. "... Then, offer to groom the person as your possible successor by teaching them your relevant skills—as long as she or he supports you."

That's really playing hardball, even for your coach, but defusing a possible enemy or troublemaker is a very pragmatic reason to help others. This is especially true if the person is qualified and only is bitter from being passed over so often. This approach applies to unhappy but worthy co-workers as well as subordinates.

················   *Coach's Tip*   ·················

Make a potential enemy into a friend by being helpful. It works.

··

If I haven't yet convinced you of the importance of helping others—and how good it feels to do so—consider this: In a workplace where teamwork is stressed and team achievements are considered a major part of the basis of evaluating each member's performance, helping others is critical. More and more, job candidates tell me that during interviews they're being asked to discuss how they feel about bringing others along, helping their colleagues and sharing information.

I found this out myself recently when I decided to test in person what it's like to go through a job interview, much like auto editors drive test cars and food writers test recipes. I wanted to hear firsthand the subtle things employers listen for that determine who gets the job—and who doesn't.

Of course, it wasn't a real interview. I arranged in advance with Grayson Mitchell, chair and CEO of Summit Consulting Group, a public affairs and public relations firm, to treat me as he would any applicant for the job of account executive. He kindly consented to take time out of his busy day to let me see what a job interview looks like up close and from the inside.

I did well in answering his questions about what I could contribute to the firm, how my bosses would describe me, some of my weaknesses (yes, I did admit to having some, but I described them as actually being strengths!) and my career goals and salary requirements.

But Grayson wanted to know some more, some pertinent information that he felt was essential to working with him and his staff that I had not yet brought up. He said, "I'm concerned about your growing people, bringing other people along. Do you consider that one of your strengths?"

What he actually wanted to hear, before considering hiring me, was whether I had a deep commitment to my co-workers, subordinates and superiors. In other words, was I an enthusiastic team player?

I assured him that I am and told him that I am, in fact, a solid team player. I've always felt that it is part of my job to help my colleagues succeed, and I enjoy enabling others to do well and advance in their careers—even beyond my professional commitment to employees and employment issues. I went on to describe my sheer delight in helping colleagues when they need it, often offering to help when no request for help is given.

I told him that when something I've suggested works or when support I've given helps co-workers feel better about themselves or do their jobs better—I feel extremely happy and satisfied. I told him that peacefully thinking about how I might have helped someone that day at work often helps get me home in one piece in the worst traffic on the worst expressways.

That's exactly what Mitchell had been waiting for. It was "symphonic music to the ears of a potential employer," he said, because such an attitude helps *him* realize his dream of "building a larger company, a bigger bottom line." The CEO said if he had been hiring, with those words of caring about my colleagues, I would have locked up the job.

················· *Coach's Tip* ················

During job interviews or other meetings with managers and clients, don't be shy about mentioning your commitment to helping others. You'll find that they feel the same way as you do.

··

My philosophy of helping others is not based on a Pollyanna, Elsie Dinsmore or Goody Two-Shoes approach to life. What it's really about is caring. And I'm not alone.

"Caring does make a difference in virtually every workplace," writes Charles Kozoll in *From Nine to Five,* a newsletter of tips and information for the office that is published by The Dartnell Corporation. Kozoll gives examples such as celebrating a colleague's birthday, offering to help out when someone's workload is too heavy and being concerned about a co-worker who is ill or recently returned from having surgery. "These actions help create a warm work atmosphere that gradually contributes to bonding, loyalty and productivity," Kozoll writes.

Here are some ways to create a caring climate, based on Kozoll's suggestions:

- Look for instances where others might need an emotional boost—and then give it to them.

- When a co-worker needs encouragement or deserves recognition, try to provide it through a phone message, E-mail, a note, a card or a kind word.

- Offer to help out whenever you can, whatever the situation. You'll find that in the future if you need help or some support, the people you've helped will extend themselves for you and eagerly will do whatever they can to help you solve the problem.

················ *Coach's Tip* ················

Be part of the office grapevine, not to try to bring people down but to learn who's in trouble and who may need your help. And then, help them.

···

Being helpful extends beyond your particular job and reaches into community, volunteer and professional groups you may be a part of. For example, a graphic designer felt she was stymied in advancing at the publishing house she worked for, so to relieve her frustration, she put her heart and soul into the activities of the national graphics association she belonged to. Soon she was invited to give speeches throughout the world about the dramatically changing world of graphics and was elected to a high office within the group.

This outside activity had an unexpected result, she said, though I wasn't the least bit surprised about it. The recognition she got on the outside was filtering back to her employers, who were delighted with the volunteer work she was doing, the positive publicity it gave them and the positive things her accomplishments said about her character and professionalism. Within a few months the graphic designer was promoted to a job she had previously applied for but had been passed over in the final selection.

· · · · · · · · · · · · · · · · *Coach's Tip* · · · · · · · · · · · · · · · ·

Good news, like bad news, always comes back to the workplace. A helpful, caring attitude in the community enhances your value in the eyes of your employer and accelerates your career advancement.

· ·

Some people find that helping other people succeed in their careers isn't enough. They want to do more. In this fashion, many employees for social agencies are born.

A young man who did volunteer work with disabled persons while in college never forgot the experience. He continued in the field he trained for as a computer operator and felt lucky to have a good-paying job with a bright future. But it wasn't enough.

All day long as he worked in cyberspace, the computer operator longed for human contact, to talk to someone in person rather than through a computer modem. After a while, he knew he had to make a change.

"I wanted to help other people, full-time," he said. He eventually left his so-called bright future to work for less pay in a job-training program for disabled adults. He looks forward to going to work every day and feels fulfilled at the end of it. "My new job may not sound as important as one in computer technology, but it *is* to the people I work with," he observed. "What I do all day long is help others. It makes me feel good."

· · · · · · · · · · · · · · · · *Coach's Tip* · · · · · · · · · · · · · · · ·

Caring people in a caring profession not only help others—they also help themselves.

· ·

When you get down to the nitty-gritty of caring about people, a real sense of caring can have the most widespread effect when it comes not from your colleagues, not from management, but from the top honchos, in particular the CEO.

And one of the ways CEOs can show they care about employees is to show they understand the importance of work and family issues. That's the kind of caring that is especially relevant to employed women, many of whom will not be able to achieve equality in the workplace unless and until important changes are made in the way work is done.

"It *can't* happen without the CEO, and it's not just a power thing but the CEO's responsibility to create values and a diverse company," said Ron Compton, chair of Aetna Life and Casualty Company, a Hartford-based insurance company with a predominantly female workforce and some of the most noteworthy family benefits in corporate America. They include flexible benefits, staggered hours, flexible hours, generous family leave, part-time jobs, job sharing, work at home, temporary jobs, child-care discounts, child- and elder-care referral, work and family seminars, support groups, mentoring and diversity awareness seminars. "I'm a realist, a pragmatist," he said. "I can figure out how to get results. You cannot let all these brilliant, well-educated people waste their talent. You have to develop it and use it."

·················· *Coach's Tip* ·················

C aring companies have loyal employees, even at a time when there is no loyalty in business. Try to get a job with a considerate firm—it will accelerate your career advancement.

··

Of course, Aetna is not the only company with a "soul." Kraft USA, an operating group of Kraft General Foods, is right up there with its career and family programs and benefits. But it is Kraft's special services for busy employees that I consider more caring than any other caring firm. They include—are you ready?—such things as take-home meals, direct-order phone line services for floral arrangements, special discounts for arts and theater, drop boxes for dry cleaning and shoe repair, gift wrapping, family resource services and a mother's room.

And there's more: on-site oil changes with no appointment necessary, video vending machines, free legal services, local merchant discounts, free Kraft products of the month, film development and travel services.

· · · · · · · · · · · · · · · · *Coach's Tip* · · · · · · · · · · · · · · · ·

The more you give, the more you get.

· ·

How does it feel to work for an organization that truly has your best interests at heart? Ask Melitta M. Budler, manager of communications at Kraft USA. Here's what she says about Kraft's career and family program and supportive style of management:

> I've personally benefited from these programs. When I became ill in 1993, Kraft approached me—and not vice versa—to tell me I was entitled to a short-term leave of absence to take care of my health. As a single parent and breadwinner, I couldn't believe my ears. When I needed a second leave in the same year, I first asked to work at home for a month. Kraft agreed and outfitted my home office with a fax. I still had to take the leave, but I was told to take the time I needed—and not to worry about my job. I felt a genuine commitment [from Kraft] to my long-term career.

Back on the job, Budler also reaps other benefits. "In terms of diversity, like other employees, I've broadened my horizons through my work on Kraft's diversity committee, participation in career day and diversity training," she says. Budler sums up the effect of a caring work atmosphere in this way: "The bottom line is these programs are a way of doing business at Kraft and provide not only flexibility and new opportunities but at times, a much-needed 'oasis' for employees like me as well."

Kraft provides the kind of work atmosphere that would have meant a lot to me when my children were small and I was raising them alone. In retrospect, if I had been employed there, I probably would have packed all my possessions, grabbed the kids and sought asylum within the friendly confines of their corporate headquarters.

·················· *Coach's Tip* ··················

Making life a bit easier for other people often means making life easier for yourself, whether you're a CEO, manager or just an everyday working person.
··

But the coin of helping others at work has a reverse side: knowing when *not* to help. You need to know what to do when it's better to keep your distance. Here are the times not to get involved:

- Not offering to help when your help clearly is not wanted

- Not getting involved when it will do you great harm, unless you feel it's so important to do something about a situation that you're willing to take a major risk to your career

- When top management strongly suggests you mind your own business

To me, helping others makes the workplace a much warmer and fuzzier place, and I try to respond to unspoken cries for help whenever I'm aware of them. Nonetheless, keep in mind that you still must respect your colleagues' right to privacy and not interfere where you aren't wanted.

·················· *Coach's Tip* ··················

Do *not* do unto others as you would *not* have them do unto you.
··

17

Preparing Yourself
for a Second Career

Even if you love what you're doing now, keep somewhere in the back of your mind that this, too, shall pass.
The U.S. Bureau of Labor Statistics projects that U.S.
workers will change careers—careers, not jobs—at least three
times over the course of their work lives.

If you hate what you're doing now, that's good news. And if
you're in a career that you suspect soon will become obsolete,
you're probably already getting ready to think about what to do
next.

················· *Coach's Tip* ·················

Whether or not by choice, you probably will not retire
doing the work you now do. And now is the time to prepare for that change.

One of the factors propelling workers to prepare themselves
for a second career is that we live longer and healthier lives. The

217

fastest-growing age group in the United States are people in their eighties, people who often are described as the "frail elderly." But many of these women and men are not frail and are working at jobs they love or in their own successful businesses.

················ *Coach's Tip* ················

You're going to live a long and, I hope, healthy and active life, so if you choose the wrong career the first time, there's plenty of time to choose a more satisfying one the second or third time around. So don't be afraid to make a change—especially since you may have no choice about it.

···

When it comes to changing careers, preparing to do so or even thinking about it—everybody's doing it! Among journalists alone, I know one who is looking into courses necessary to become a high school teacher; another who currently is studying to become a registered nurse; a third who has completed the course work necessary to start her own design consulting firm (I was her first happy and satisfied paying client); and another who, after working as a reporter and going to law school at night for several years, now is a successful lawyer with a prestigious position on the staff of the local state attorney's office.

Among my friends who are not journalists (and, yes, I do have some), I know one dental hygienist also studying to be a nurse and another who recently became a dentist, a paralegal who is enrolled in law school, a retail sales executive preparing for a career in cooking and catering, and a real estate salesperson studying to become an accountant.

And of some of the people I've recently interviewed on other subjects, a former truck driver now is a Teamsters' Union official, a former high-powered public relations executive who was "downsized" by a large corporation now heads a social services agency, a former teacher has started an educational publishing firm specializing in crafts, a job coach for the disabled is studying to be a clinical psychologist and a former officer with the U.S. Navy heads a diversity program at an engineering institute to recruit and retain young women as science and engineering students.

················ *Coach's Tip* ················

If you start early to think about beginning a new career, you won't be surprised when the time comes and you *have* to make a change. Or, even better, you'll be ready to make a change simply because you want to do something different, something you really want to pursue.

··

The point I'm emphasizing here as your coach is that your first career won't be your last. Understanding that is part of the flexibility you must have to survive in the labor market of the 21st century. Now is the time to flex your flexibility muscles and prepare for "serial" careers, whether you're just starting out in the work world, are a seasoned professional or even retired.

Phyllis Moen, a Cornell University sociologist quoted in the *Chicago Tribune*, says the typical pattern of school, work and then retirement may become outmoded as lifestyles continue to change. Not only will women who are wives and mothers—traditionally expected to stay home and take care of husbands and children—continue to flood the labor market, but people will continue to work beyond the traditional retirement age of 65 years, probably in completely different fields. And even those who do retire, at any age, will continue to change professions, starting second, third and fourth careers after retiring.

················ *Coach's Tip* ················

Changing careers is not something that only older or retired people will be doing. You may find after being out of school only a few years that the profession you trained for has been replaced by a smart machine that can do the work. Young and old alike have to be prepared at any time to start something new.

··

For instance, take Debi Thomas, a former Olympic figure skater who won a bronze medal in Calgary's 1988 Olympics. She used her figure skating skills to earn money for medical school and now, at the age of 26, is studying to be a doctor. It's true that Thomas could not be a champion athlete all her life—no one can because of the inevitable deterioration of physical skills. But she didn't wait for that day to come. She prepared for it well in advance and is making a comfortable transition to something she loves as much as skating.

················· *Coach's Tip* ·················

Don't fight the idea of having to do something different from what you're now doing. Instead, embrace the opportunity to start all over again and to do something well.
··

I frequently hear stories about employees whose present bosses actually ask them to switch professions. After first being somewhat taken aback, most are pleased and flattered. When the boss asks you to make a change, you know the company is behind you while you're learning new skills. You also know that while others may lose their jobs in continual cutbacks, you will not be one of them. You know, too, that you are filling a new and necessary slot and are safe, at least for the time being.

················· *Coach's Tip* ·················

Don't be too surprised when your employer asks you to stop what you're doing and learn an entirely new discipline. Or you might even want to suggest doing so yourself, if you see the need.
··

Some of the corporate switches are surprising. For instance, International Business Machines Corporation (IBM), the beleaguered computer manufacturer, recently put a former Nabisco marketing executive in charge of its huge personal computer operations. The move is not an isolated one. According to *The Wall Street Journal*, the move "comes amid a spate of similar moves through the technology world. Engineers and programmers are being nudged aside and packaged-goods experts are the hot new commodity as PC and software companies attempt to fashion brand names out of products that are looking more and more alike."

·············· **Coach's Tip** ···············

If you're an engineer or programmer who hopes to head your firm's computer operations someday, now may be a good time to think of recareering.
···

And if you feel that switching from one career to another is an awful lot to handle, consider this: You may not be able to switch to just one career to earn a living. You may have to learn several new skills and piece them together in order to earn a living.

Wendy Reid Crisp, writing in *Executive Female* and quoted in *ReCareering Magazine,* the excellent newsletter for career switchers published by Sharon B. Schuster, calls what some of us might have to do to get by in today's labor market "casserole careers." Crisp says, "We have accepted the concept of serial careers. . . . Now we have patchwork careers. Or maybe it's 'casserole careers'—a little bit of cheese, some bacon, a few slices of day-old bread. . . . Fewer and fewer of us can earn a living from a single source."

·············· **Coach's Tip** ···············

The people whom we call *moonlighters,* who earn their living from working several jobs, usually a full-time one during the day and a part-time one nights and weekends, most often moonlight to make enough money to put food on the table. But they also may be the people best prepared to ease into a second career when the time comes.
···

Crisp describes preparing for a second career as "the mix of our ambitions and our cleverness, the ability to piece together work that will both satisfy and support us." She emphasizes that "it's the secret to surviving, even thriving. . . ."

Start right now to think about what you would do if you weren't doing what you do now. Here are some warm-up exercises to prepare for recareering:

- *Retake the quiz in Chapter 1 about what is the right job for you.* It will also help you ascertain what gives you a sense of gratification and accomplishment and what your interests are.

- *Retake the quiz in Chapter 15.* Determine your happiness quotient, what you want to get out of a new career—and what you want to avoid next time.

- *Look at the list in the back of this book of the 100 best jobs for the 1990s and beyond.* Is what you want to do in a field with a future? While you're at it, check the current and projected salaries.

- *When you find something that fascinates you—and you shouldn't settle for anything less—do your homework.* Find out everything you can about the field. How long does it take to become qualified? What are the best schools to go to or courses to take to prepare for the career switch? Will you be able to learn the necessary skills while holding down your present job? What companies hire people in the field? Where are they located?

- *Start talking to people in the field and learn about it from the inside.* Before making a commitment to it, use your weekends and vacation time to serve an internship, work part-time or do volunteer work—anything to get you inside—in your new field. See if you like it. You may not. If you do, you will not only be energized by knowing that your next step will be something you will enjoy; you also will have established important networking contacts.

· · · · · · · · · · · · · · · · *Coach's Tip* · · · · · · · · · · · · · · · ·

If you decide on a particular field, one of the first things you should do, even before signing up for any courses or further education, is to go to the library and carefully study the *Encyclopedia of Associations,* the valuable reference tool that lists all professional groups.

● ●

Find several associations in your area of interest and contact them. Decide which one is best for you to join, based on how much information it will give you on how to become qualified for the work, what the roadblocks might be, if it will help you find a mentor in your city—and if it has a job bank.

I stress the importance of figuring out how much time it will take and what it will cost to start a new career because there are very few careers you automatically can segue into. In fact, the only one I can think of is for a lawyer to become an actor, because so many of the same skills are required. But even the most brilliant trial lawyers still would need a few basic acting classes.

● ● ● ● ● ● ● ● ● ● ● ● ● ● ● ● ●   *Coach's Tip*   ● ● ● ● ● ● ● ● ● ● ● ● ● ● ● ●

Don't make any sudden moves. Instead, write down your one-year to five-year plan to start a new career.

● ●

In your plan, estimate how long it will take you to make the change. Allocate the money necessary for you to become qualified. Factor in that you will probably be working in your present job while preparing for your new career.

Here are more tips to ensure the success of your second career:

- *Talk to a private career counselor or community college, four-year college or university placement officer.* What courses will you need? What credit will you get for what you already know? How long will the process take? How to study on your own? Where are the jobs?

- *Play it by ear at work as far as whether you tell your boss or colleagues what you are doing.* If you're unemployed or retired, this isn't a problem. But if you're working, you don't want to jeopardize your livelihood. On the other

hand, some firms look very favorably on people who prepare themselves for new careers. And you might even
qualify for tuition reimbursement.

- *Education, education, education.* As you may have guessed
  by now, I'm a strong advocate for education. And I do
  think that people who switch careers have to prove they
  are qualified far more than someone who prepared for the
  same field the first time around. That's why I urge career
  changers to get every advanced certification and creden-
  tial available to show that you know your stuff.

· · · · · · · · · · · · · · · · · *Coach's Tip* · · · · · · · · · · · · · · · · ·

If you've been thinking of switching from a job in a nonprofit organization to a for-profit one, or the other way
around, now is a good time to do so.

· ·

Volunteer work is the secret to making that change. If you're
currently working at a nonprofit agency, get to know the people
on the board of directors. They're usually from the for-profit sector. Or if you want to be part of a caring organization, do volunteer work in that organization. You'll not only find out if it's
your right choice for a second career, but you'll also make important contacts in the field and will be the first to know of any
openings that arise.

· · · · · · · · · · · · · · · · · *Coach's Tip* · · · · · · · · · · · · · · · · ·

One of the factors involved in serial careers is, of course,
salary. Unfortunately, you may have to settle for less. At
least at first.

· ·

Career changers who start at an entry-level position may have
unrealistic salary expectations. "Career changers sometimes
expect salaries at or near their previous wage," said Jamie King,

associate director of graduate business services at the University of Texas/Austin. Quoted in *Recruiting Trends,* a monthly newsletter for recruiting executives, King asserts that most likely you will not match your previous wages. She suggests to employers that they should explain to career switchers the reasons for offering an entry-level salary and provide an estimate of how long it will take you to get raises and promotions.

················ *Coach's Tip* ················

Be realistic about what salary to expect in a new career and what your chances are to move ahead. You may be new at the profession, but your greatest advantage is that you have a much clearer idea of the job you want and are much better focused than new college graduates.

··

However, the playing field is not always level. Despite age discrimination laws, older people have a harder time getting a job after switching careers than younger people. And "older" may even start at age 35, though the people I hear complaints from most often are job seekers in a new field who are 50 years and over. "I'm trying to make a mid-life career change," a teacher wrote me. "I tried three different agencies to help me get interviews, but nothing happened. What can I do?"

Thousands of women and men change careers after age 50—a time of life described by Dr. Lydia Bronte, a former director of the Aging Society Project at Carnegie Corporation and author of *The Longevity Factor* (HarperCollins), as "a major peak of creativity, in many cases lasting for 25 or 30 years" thereafter. But the secret to their success is that they do it themselves. That's why I advised the teacher to forget agencies that work only for employers, not clients, and to pick a field for herself and do her own job hunting.

I told the teacher that from her letter and resume she might do well in the hospitality industry, especially as a travel agent, or in sales, especially in selling educational books and videos. I urged her to take it from there.

················ *Coach's Tip* ················

No matter what age you are, you have to know what profession you want to enter. No one will do it for you.
··

Recently I chose 12 best jobs for people over 50 for *New Choices*, a magazine for retirement living. In making my selections, I looked for growing fields that require relatively short training courses, value life and work experience and offer secure incomes and possibilities for advancement. The professions included chef/cook, computer systems analyst, graphic design, insurance sales, interior design, paralegal, personnel training/labor relations, public relations, real estate sales, registered nursing, travel agency and veterinary technician.

················ *Coach's Tip* ················

When you decide it's time to make a change, don't consider staying in your profession but at a lower level because of your age. That's discriminating against yourself, and you can do better.
··

A lawyer called me to tell me he had been edged out of his law firm at age 40, without ever making partner. Though he had seen the handwriting on the wall, he had not prepared for it. "But I have a good idea," he told me. "I'm going to look for work as a paralegal. I'd be good at it, because as a lawyer, I know exactly what lawyers want."

I told him it probably was a good time to switch careers, but becoming a paralegal was not the answer. "It's a hard, technical job, and you will not be able to do it without getting additional training," I said. "And after you get it, there's little reason to think a law firm would hire a lawyer to do the job, even if you were willing to accept the low pay the position pays."

Instead, I suggested that he bite the bullet and think of doing something a little different. Why not start a temporary firm that provides paralegals? In that business, he would indeed know exactly what lawyers want. What about supplying court reporters, another growth field? He seemed interested in those ideas and added that perhaps becoming a paralegal wasn't the best solution.

·············· *Coach's Tip* ················

One of the best second, third or even fourth careers is to start your own business.

···

The joke in the 1980s was that anyone who was fired called themselves a consultant. In the 1990s and the 21st century, being a consultant is an excellent transition from a job working for someone else to starting your own business and becoming your own boss. Many people start doing consulting work while in their present jobs, hoping to collect enough accounts to become full-time entrepreneurs.

·············· *Coach's Tip* ················

When your present boss says, "Thanks, but you're fired," it may be the time to explore starting your own firm.

···

Professional athletes, including football, baseball and basketball players and even former sumo wrestlers, often start their own restaurants. Artists start their own graphic design firms. Sales representatives open their own stores. Anyone connected in any way with computers becomes a high-tech consultant. Former government employees open their own research firms. Editors start their own desktop publishing firms, often beginning with newsletters. The examples are endless.

Here are some tips for getting started:

- Make sure that you have an idea for a service that is needed and that you think you can provide better than anyone else.

- Draw up a marketing plan that includes your costs, potential clients, potential suppliers and how long it will take you to make a profit.

- Get all the advice you can from people already in the business, from agencies that provide entrepreneurial advice and from bankers and friends or from books about becoming an entrepreneur.

- Take courses in business management, in how to start a new business. Don't make a move until you have the expertise you need.

- Join your local chamber of commerce or other business groups for advice and support.

- After you've done your homework, start visiting banks to see if you will be able to borrow money. If they turn you down, start visiting friends and relatives. Don't make the mistake of being underfinanced, not only in start-up money but for capital investments for expansion when things go well.

- Start small but think big. Keep expenditures as low as possible by starting from home and with as few employees as possible.

- At the end of your first year, evaluate how you're doing and what your chances are for continued success. Most new businesses fail in their first year, so if you've lasted that long, you're doing well.

··············· *Coach's Tip* ················

Starting a new career as an entrepreneur makes it hard ever to work for anyone else again. You have now become the boss, and that's very different from becoming an employee.

······································

I urge anyone who can do so to start their own business, as each of my children has done. However, if you prefer to work for someone else or have no choice about it, make sure it's the best possible job you can get, the right job for you, whether it's your first, second or third career. Your coach wants you to be successful in whatever you do.

·················· *Coach's Tip* ··················

Go for it!

··

Appendix A
Where To Go for More Information

BOOKS

America's Changing Workforce. Nuventures Consultants, 1989.

Andler, Edward. *Winning the Hiring Game: Reference & Employee Background Checks in the 1990s . . . A New Approach.* Smith Collins, 1994.

Bard, Ray, and Susan K. Elliott. *National Directory of Corporate Training Programs.* Doubleday, 1989.

Beatty, Richard. *The Complete Job Search Book.* Wiley, 1991.

Boyett, Joseph, and Henry Conn. *Workplace: The Revolution Reshaping American Business.* Dutton, 1990.

Butler, Joel. *High Technology Degree Alternatives: Earning a High-Tech Degree While Working Full-Time.* Professional Publications, Inc., 1994.

Careers Tomorrow. World Future Society, 1990.

CEIP Fund. *The Complete Guide to Environmental Careers.* Island Press, 1990.

Cohen, Lilly, and Dennis Young. *Careers for Dreamers and Doers: A Guide to Management Careers in the Nonprofit Sector.* The Foundation Center, 1991.

Dictionary of Occupational Titles, 2 vols. U.S. Department of Labor, 1992.

Feingold, Norman, and Maxine Atwater. *New Emerging Careers.* Garrett Park Press, 1990.

Ferguson, Trudi, and Joan Dunphy. *Answers to the Mommy Track: How Wives and Mothers in Business Reach the Top and Balance Their Lives.* New Horizons Press, 1991.

Fry, Ron. *101 Great Answers to the Toughest Interview Questions.* Career Press, 1992.

Geoghegan, Thomas. *Which Side Are You On? Trying To Be for Labor When It's Flat on Its Back*. Farrar, Strauss & Giroux, 1991.

Harkavy, Michael. *101 Careers: A Guide to the Fastest-Growing Opportunities*. Wiley, 1990.

Harrison, Bennett, and Barry Bluestone. *The Great U-Turn: Corporate Restructuring and the Polarizing of America*. Basic Books, 1989.

Heuer, Albert. *Moving Up the Corporate Ladder: All You Need To Know To Make the Climb*. Small Business Press, 1990.

Hoover, Gary, et al. *Hoover's Handbook of World Business*. Reference Press, 1993.

Hyatt, Carole. *Shifting Gears*. Simon & Schuster, 1991.

Kanter, Donald, and Philip Mirvis. *The Cynical American: Living and Working in an Age of Discontent and Disillusion*. Jossey-Bass, 1991.

Kanter, Rosabeth Moss. *When Giants Learn To Dance: Mastering the Challenges of Strategy*. Simon & Schuster, 1989.

Kleiman, Carol. *The 100 Best Jobs for the 1990s & Beyond*. Dearborn Financial Publishing, Inc., 1992.

Kneffel Daniels, Peggy, and Carol A. Schwartz, editors. *Encyclopedia of Associations*. Gale Publishing, 1994.

Krantz, Les. *The Jobs-Rated Almanac*. World Almanac, 1990.

Laqueur, Maria, and Donna Dickinson. *Breaking Out of 9 to 5: How To Redesign Your Job To Fit You*. Peterson's, 1994.

Norback, Craig. *VGM's Careers Encyclopedia*. VGM Career Horizons, 1991.

Occupational Outlook Handbook, 1993–94. U.S. Department of Labor, Bureau of Labor Statistics.

Opportunity 2000: Creative Affirmative Action Strategies for a Changing Workforce. Hudson Institute, for the U.S. Department of Labor, 1988.

Sibbald, John. *The New Career Makers: The Book That Leads You to the Power Brokers Who Can Advance Your Career—and Land New Talent for Your Organization*. Harper Business, 1994.

Silvestri, George, and John Lukasiewicz. *Projections 2000: A Look at Occupational Employment in the Year 2000*. Division of Occupational Outlook, U.S. Department of Labor, Bureau of Labor Statistics, September 1987.

Swanson, Barbara. *Careers in Health Care*. VGM Career Horizons, 1991.

Sweeney, John, and Karen Nussbaum. *Solutions for the New Work Force: Policies for a New Social Contract*. Seven Locks Press, 1990.

Tepper, Ron. *Power Resumes*. Wiley, 1992.

Watanuki, Kumiko. *Business and Career Planning Workbook*. Vantage Press, 1990.

Wegmann, Chapman and Johnson. *Work in the New Economy*. American Association for Counseling and Development, 1990.

Workforce America: Managing Employee Diversity as a Vital Resource. Irwin Professional Publishing, 1990.

Workforce 2000: Work and Workers for the 21st Century. Hudson Institute, for the U.S. Department of Labor, 1987.

Working in America: A Chart Book. U.S. Department of Labor, 1987.

Woy, Patricia. *Small Businesses That Grow and Grow and Grow.* Betterway Publications, 1990.

Wright, John, and Edward Dwyer. *The American Almanac of Jobs and Salaries.* Avon, 1990.

NEWSLETTERS, MAGAZINES AND JOURNALS

Kleiman, Carol. "The Best Jobs Now for People over 50." *New Choices.* May 1994.

Occupational Outlook Quarterly, U.S. Department of Labor, Bureau of Labor Statistics, Fall 1993 special issue on "The American Work Force: 1992–2005."

ReCareering Newsletter (Publications Plus, Inc., 801 Skokie Blvd., Suite 221, Northbrook, IL 60062; 708-498-1981). Published 10 times a year.

Recruiting Trends (Remy Publishing Co., 350 W. Hubbard St., Suite 440, Chicago, IL 60610; 312-464-0300). Monthly newsletter for the recruiting executive.

"The 25 Hottest Careers," "The Best—and Worst—Jobs for Women," "How To Ace a Tough Interview," "Five Cold Hard Facts about the Job Market Now," "Switching Careers the Smartest Way," *Working Woman.* July 1994.

··

Appendix B
The 100 Best Jobs in the 1990s and Beyond

Salaries are one of the best-kept secrets in the U.S. labor market. But without accurate salary information, you have very little power in wage negotiation. Such information is essential to plan your career, to keep it moving along and, above all, to make sure that you are being paid fairly. The jobs below show you the current salaries and projected salaries for the year 2000. The current salaries are average or salary ranges unless otherwise indicated.

The 100 top jobs listed in this appendix fall into one of the following 10 categories:

1. Business and Financial Services

2. Education, Government and Social Services

3. Engineering and Computer Technology

4. Health Care Professions

5. Hospitality Industry

6. Management and Office Personnel

7. Manufacturing, Repair, Construction, Agriculture and Transportation

8. Media and the Arts

9. Sales and Personal Services

10. Science

Jobs were chosen based on information from the U.S. Department of Labor and its *Monthly Labor Review,* from my own research and daily coverage of employment and from interviews with career counselors, leaders of professional associations, economists and human resource executives. I have omitted occupations that are just work, not careers with a future. I have included a sprinkling of jobs that don't require college or graduate degrees but do have great potential as entry-level jobs or can lead to future entrepreneurship. For more detailed information, see *The 100 Best Jobs for the 1990s & Beyond* (Chicago: Dearborn Financial Publishing, Inc., 1992).

Job	Salary Mid-1990s	Salary (Projected) Year 2000
Accountant/Auditor	$28,000**	$43,000*
Actor/Director/Producer		
Actor	6,614–100,000+	12,000–150,000+
Director	38,587–100,000+	70,000–200,000+
Producer	66,150–100,000+	95,000–200,000+
Advertising and Marketing Account Supervisor	45,000–67,000	70,000
Agricultural Scientist	20,189–22,150**	45,000*
Aircraft Technician	32,500	30,000–45,000
Appliance/Power Tool Repairer	24,281	40,000
Architect	36,700	61,596
Arts Administrator	22,700*	50,000*
Automotive Mechanic	21,216	36,000
Bank Loan Officer	27,000–44,000	40,000–65,000*
Bank Marketer	28,000–156,000	50,000–300,000
Biological Scientist	34,500	50,000
Carpenter	22,100	34,650
Chemist	24,000*	64,000*
Clerical Supervisor/Office Manager	21,100–39,400	25,000–60,000
Commercial & Graphic Artist	23,000	35,000
Computer Operator	16,000–28,700	33,000–42,000

Job	Salary Mid-1990s	Salary (Projected) Year 2000
Computer Programmer	$35,600	$52,632
Computer Service Technician	32,708	52,000
Computer Systems Analyst	32,200–52,200	48,000–67,000
Cook/Chef		
Cook	13,000*	26,000*
Chef	40,000*	60,000*
Corporate Financial Analyst	20,200–77,800	101,400
Corporate Personnel Trainer	32,000	50,000
Corrections Officer/Guard/Jailer	23,200	21,000–35,000
Cosmetologist	20,000–30,000	18,000
Court Reporter	19,240–28,080	37,000
Database Manager	35,000–80,000	50,000
Dental Hygienist	31,668	39,800
Dentist	90,000	125,000
Dietitian	28,500	40,000–80,000
Drafter	20,600–35,100	20,000–60,000
Economist	25,200***	40,512***
Editor/Writer	20,000–60,000	50,000
Educational Administrator	45,400–63,000	70,000
Employment Interviewer	17,000–25,000	25,000–48,000*
Engineer	34,000**	68,000**
Environmental Scientist	22,717–33,623*	68,200*
Farm Manager	19,864	30,000
Financial Planner	39,700	30,000–50,000*
Firefighter	33,072	42,000
Flight Attendant	20,000–40,000	34,000–53,422
Flight Engineer	42,000	65,000
Food Scientist	25,000*	35,000*
Health Services Administrator	46,600–166,700	71,250
Home Health Aide	13,800	20,000
Hotel Manager/Assistant	32,500–59,100	80,000+
Human Resources Manager/ Executive	76,900	122,160
Industrial Designer	27,900*	45,000*
Information Systems Manager	50,000–100,000	225,250
Insurance Claim Examiner	22,360	32,260
Insurance Salesperson	30,100	86,400
Interior Designer	25,000–38,000	47,000+

Job	Salary Mid-1990s	Salary (Projected) Year 2000
Investment Banker	$40,300	$77,000–86,000*
Labor Relations Specialist	32,000	61,818
Landscape Architect	20,400***	35,000–42,600*
Lawyer	36,000–134,000	88,000
Librarian	23,800–45,200	40,300–124,000
Licensed Practical Nurse	21,476	42,000
Management Consultant	40,300	60,000–72,000
Manufacturing Specialist (CAD/ CAM and CAI)	34,000	45,000
Mathematician/Statistician	29,400***	45,000***
Medical Records Administrator	47,600	64,000
Occupational Therapist	35,625	51,000
Office/Business Machine Repairer	24,752	37,565
Operations Manager/ Manufacturing	60,000	95,000
Operations/Systems Research Analyst	50,000	62,500
Ophthalmic Laboratory Technician	15,040–24,370	16,785–26,000
Optician	26,000	40,000
Paralegal	28,300	39,840
Paramedic	28,079	36,000
Peripheral Electronic Data Processing Equipment Operator	21,000	30,000
Pharmacist	45,000	60,605
Photographer/Camera Operator	21,200	35,882
Physical Therapist	35,464	45,000–96,000
Physician	170,600	233,906
Physician Assistant	41,038	47,250
Physicist/Astronomer	30,000*	62,000*
Pilot	80,000	125,000
Podiatrist	35,578*–119,674	68,412*
Police Officer	32,000	42,750
Psychologist/Counselor	35,000–55,000	45,000–75,000
Public Relations Specialist	32,000	50,000
Radio/TV News Reporter	17,000–41,000	44,000*
Radio/TV Service Technician	25,168	24,000–35,000
Radiologic Technologist	28,236	41,000*
Real Estate Agent/Broker	16,796–41,706	46,200+

Job	Salary Mid-1990s	Salary (Projected) Year 2000
Real Estate Appraiser	$26,364	$50,000
Registered Nurse	34,424	50,000*
Reporter/Correspondent	16,000–69,500	30,000–100,000
Restaurant/Food Service Manager	27,900–45,000	65,000
Retail Salesperson	13,260–24,908	20,000–27,000
Secretary/Office Administrator	26,700	24,000
Social Worker	20,000–30,000	45,000
Speech Pathologist/Audiologist	36,036	46,000
Teacher/Professor		
Teacher	34,800–36,000	46,733
Professor	27,700–59,500	71,211
Travel Agent	12,428*–25,007	27,000
Truck Driver	20,000–40,000	24,000–35,000
Underwriter	30,576	45,427
Veterinarian	27,858*–63,069	34,000*
Wholesale Sales Representative	32,000	40,000

   * = indicates starting salary
  ** = indicates salary with bachelor's degree
*** = indicates starting salary with bachelor's degree

Index

A

Abusive managers, 97–109
  discussing with personnel rep, 100
  job search in connection with, 101
  reacting to, 102–3
Advertising
  blind ads, 41, 43
  job classifieds, 28–29
  yourself, 30
Aetna Life and Casualty Company, 213
Affirmative action, 94
  myth of, 95
African Americans, in workforce, 95
  minority discrimination, 45, 118, 150
Age discrimination, 225
Alltritten, Drew, 185–86
Alliances, 118
Ameritech, 84
Anecdotal resume, 17
Antidiscrimination laws, 95, 151
Antinepotism rules, 123
Appearance
  during job interview, 46–47
  on job, 78–79

Aptitude tests, 47
Aristotle, 189
Arthur Andersen & Co., 184
Asian Americans, in workforce, 94
Associations, professional, 23
Attitude, 59, 75

B

Benefits, 36–37, 44–45, 65
Blind ads, 41, 43
Bonding with co-workers, 118–19
Bonuses, 137
  at end of severance period, 158
Breaking Out of 9 to 5: How to Redesign Your Job to Fit You, 197
Bronte, Lydia, 225
Budler, Melitta M., 214
Burnett, Leo, 92
Business
  books, 36
  clubs, 24

C

Cafeteria benefits, 37
Cantrell, Will, 32
Career changes, 217–29
  consulting, 227
  education and, 224
  older workers, 225–26

starting your own business,
227–29
volunteer work, 224
warm-up exercises, 222
Career counselors, 6, 25
Career guidance, in community
colleges, 31
Certified mail, and resume
distribution, 43
Character, of job applicant, 19
Chemical industry, 45
Chicago Tribune, 86
Child care referral services, 37
Civil Rights Act, 51
Classified ads, 28–29
Collaboration, 87–88
College placement centers, 24, 31
Communicating your needs, 125–38
applying for posted jobs,
128–30
performance reviews, 130–33
salary reviews, 133–37
Community colleges, 31
Community work, 148
Comparable worth laws, 136
Compton, Ron, 213
Computer literacy, 179–80
Conferences, 137
Confidence, 71–72
Conflict management, 102. *See also*
Abusive managers
Consultants
career, 24–25
for former employers, 155–56
as second career, 227
Contingency workers, 89–90
Continuing education, 179–89
employee compensation for,
181
older students and, 185
technology and, 179–80
Cooperation, 148. *See also* Teamwork
Cooperative education, 10, 33
Counselors, for career advice, 6, 25
Counteroffers, salary, 65
Cover letters, with resumes, 19–21
Crying, 201–2

Currently employed workers
giving notice, 68
job searches and, 37–38

D

Day-care centers, on site, 37
Details, organizing, 111–12
Dickinson, Donna, 197
Discrimination
abusive managers and, 101
age, 225
antidiscrimination laws, 95, 120
club memberships and, 118
confronting and reporting,
120–22
employment lawyers and, 155
-in-hiring lawsuit, 47
in promotions, 150
psychological tests and, 48
recording practices of, 120
sex, 91
Discussion groups, 24
Diversity in workforce, 46, 93–95,
213
Documented Reference Check, 60
Downsizings, 61
Driver, Michael J., 86

E

Egan, Gerard R., 74, 85
Elder-care, 37
E-mail, 117
Employee handbook, 74, 156
Employment
agencies, 34
office, state, 30
Employment at will, 156–57
Enthusiasm, 75
Entry-level jobs, 12
distinguishing yourself in, 145
management training
programs, 84–85
Equal Employment Office, 121
Equal Pay Act, 136
Erdlen, Jack, 41–42
Evaluations, 76–77
Executive recruiters, 34
Exit interviews, 160

F

Fairfax Hospital, 151
Family benefits, 36–37
Family and Medical Leave Act
 (FMLA), 36, 198
Family oriented companies, 44–45
Featherstone, Harry E., 185
Federal education reimbursement
 plan, 181
Financial condition of company, 53
Firing, 153–163
 exit interview, 160
 exit strategy after, 155–56
 health benefits and, 158
 obtaining letter of reference,
  157–58
 outplacement services, 159
 severance pay, 158, 162–63
 unemployment compensation,
  158, 162–63
Flamboyance, 23
Flexibility, 8–9, 75, 112
Flexible hours, 37, 197
Focus, 142
Follow-up calls, 55, 62
Full financial disclosure, 157
Functional resume, 17

G

Giving notice, 68
Glass ceiling, 91, 94, 151
Golfing, 118
Goods-producing sector, 81
Gossip, 73
Grapevine, 73, 211
Grooming. *See* Appearance
Grunt work, 12

H

Happiness quotient, 191–202
 exercise, 193–94
 leadership skills, 198–99
 personal time, 196
 reality check, 194–95
 recognition for work, 199
 window views and, 193
Harley-Davidson, 86
Headhunters, 34

Health benefits, 158
Health care, 10
Helping others, 205–15
 CEO and company values, 213
 colleagues, 210
 creating a caring climate, 211
 grooming your replacement,
  208
 reciprocity, 206
 teamwork, 209–10
 volunteer work, 212
Hirsch, Arlene S., 50
Hispanics, in workforce, 94–95
Historical resume, 17
Home, working from, 149
Homework
 for current job, 146
 job search, 27–38, 44, 161
 salary reviews, 134

I

Information Age, 86, 184
Informational interviews, 9–10
Information technology, 87
In-house networks, 118, 174–75. *See
 also* Networking
Initiative, 75
Integrative management style, 86
International Employment Hotline, 32
Internships, 10, 33
Interview. *See* Job interview
Intuition, 152

J

Jirak, Mary Ann, 146
Job banks, 30, 31
Job clubs, 33–34
Job fairs, 33
Job-hop, 60–62
Job interview, 43–55
 appearance and, 46
 aptitude/skills tests, 47
 early arrival to, 47
 follow-up to, 55, 62
 humor during, 49
 "job-hopping" concerns, 60–62
 multiple, for single position,
  58–59

"overqualified" candidates,
57–58
personal/illegitimate questions
during, 50–51
psychological tests, 47–48
questions to ask interviewer,
52–53
requesting, 43–44
researching prospective
employer, 44
submitting work samples, 54–55
time, 49
types of questions asked, 50–51
Job offers, 63–68
employment agreements, 67–68
employment contracts, 67
relocation considerations, 66–67
salary negotiations, 63–65
Job postings, 128–30, 145
Job satisfaction. *See* Happiness
quotient
Job scams, 31, 207
Job search
see also Career changes
homework and, 27–38
organizing, 39–40
as reaction to abusive manager,
101
while currently employed,
37–38, 41–42, 128–30
Job security, 88, 90
Job sharing, 37

K
Kaplan, Rachel, 193
Keeping current, 71–81
changes in workplace, 74–75,
80–81
employee handbook, 74
homework, 71–74
office grapevine, 73
office politics, 79–80
teamwork, 75–77
written and unwritten rules, 74
Kennedy, Marilyn Moats, 126
Kennedy's Career Strategist, 126
King, Jamie, 224–25

Kozoll, Charles, 210
Kraft General Foods, 213–15

L
Laqueur, Maria, 197
Lateral moves, 146–47
Layoffs, 61
Leave of absence, 36–37
Letter of reference, 157–58
Lindquist, Victor R., 12–13
List making, 112
Longevity Factor, 225
Low profile, in early days of job,
72–73

M
Magazines, professional, 36, 137
Mall of America, 184
Management training programs,
84–85
Managers, 83–95, 113
abusive. *See* Abusive managers
contingency workers and,
89–90
creating collaborative team
spirit, 87
integrative management style,
86
job security and, 88, 90
management training
programs, 84–85
middle managers, 83–84
secretarial staff and, 90–91
staff diversity, acknowledging,
93–95
staffing responsibilities, 89
and technology, 87
women as, 91–92
Master of business administration,
85–86, 87
Medea, Andra, 102, 104
Mentors, 115–17, 129, 145–46
Mergers, 154
Middle managers, 83–84, 154
Minorities, and job discrimination,
45, 118, 150
Mitchell, Grayson, 209
Motorola University, 184

N

National Board for Certified Counselors, 25
Negative references, 60
Nepotism, 123
Networking, 23, 29, 165–77
    confidentiality in, 172
    general organization, 173
    in-house, 174–75
    for mentors, 117
    and other organized activities compared, 168
    professional organization, 173
    setting up your own network, 176–77
Networks, for online resume distribution, 18
New Career Makers, The, 34
Newly-hired. *See* Keeping current
Newsletters, 137
Nonprofit organizations, volunteering for, 10

O

Offers. *See* Job offers
Office grapevine, 73, 211
Office politics, 79–80
Office romances, 122–23
Office Team, 199
Older workers
    age discrimination, 225
    best jobs for people over 50, 226
100 Best Jobs for the 1990s & Beyond, The, 194
Online
    distribution of resumes, 18
    finding mentors with, 117
    networks, 32–33
Organizing for success, 111–23
    alliances with colleagues, 118
    avoiding office romances, 122–23
    day-to-day details, 111–12
    dealing with discrimination/nepotism, 120–23
    flexibility in, 112
    in-house networking, 118–19
    mentors, 115–177
    teamwork and, 114–15
Outplacement consultants, 35, 159
"Overqualified" job candidates, 57–58
Overseas employment, 31–32, 150

P–Q

Partnership Group, 45
Part-time jobs, 33, 42
Pay equity, 136
Pay for performance, 134. *See also* Salary
Performance reviews, 91, 106, 130–33
Perks, 66
Personal questions, during job interview, 50–51
Personnel records, right to review, 106
Photos, in resumes, 22
Placement centers, college, 24
Plous, Jeanne M., 202
Politics, office, 79–80
Private consultants, 24–25
Preemployment psychological test, 47
Pregnancy Discrimination Act, 198
Professional associations, 23–24, 148. *See also* Networking
    mentors and, 117
Professional magazines, 36, 137
Professional Secretaries International, 90
Prototype resume, 16
Psychological tests, 47–48
Publishing industry, 45
Quality of life, as job requirement, 36. *See also* Happiness quotient

R

Rado, Stuart Alan, 25, 207–8
Raises, 65–66, 133–37
Recareering. *See* Career changes
ReCareering Newsletter, 186
Recruiting Trends, 225
References, 22
    confidentiality and, 41

dealing with negative, 60
letter of reference, requesting,
157–58
Reich, Robert B., 113
Rejection, attitude toward, 59
Relocating, 42, 66–67
Researching marketplace, 80
Restructuring, 154
Resume, 15–25
color of, 17
cover letter with, 19–21
creativity in, 130
flamboyant delivery of, 23
follow-up calls, 43–44
functional, historical, or
anecdotal, 17
online distribution of, 18
photo with, 22
prototype, 16
references, 22
salary requirements
unmentioned in, 22
sending, 39, 43
truthfulness of, 18, 19
video, 18, 22
Retraining, 180
Rigdon, Joan E., 208
Romances with co-workers, 122–23

S

St. James, Elaine, 191
Salary
benefits as part of package, 65
counteroffer, 65
freezes, 134
negotiating, 63–65
projections, 144
requirements unmentioned in
resume, 22
researching, 64
reviews, 65–66, 133–37
Salespeople, attitude toward
rejection, 59
Scams, 31, 207
Sculley, John, 53
Second career, preparing for. *See*
Career changes

Secretarial staff, 90–91, 136
discrimination against, 150,
200–201
Security, 88, 90
Self-employed workers, 81
returning to structured
employment, 200
starting a business, 227–29
Self-examination, 4–5
Self-Placement Network, Inc., 32
Self-starters, 75
Seminars, 137
Service-producing sector, 81, 162,
179
Severance pay, 158, 162–63
Sex discrimination, 51, 91, 120–22,
123
Sexual harassment, 120–22
Sibbald, John, 34
Simplify Your Life, 191
Skills tests, 47
Special projects, volunteering for,
147
Starting your own business, 227–29
State employment office, 30
Stone, Arthur, 192
Stool pigeons, 107–8
Strategic Outsourcing, 41
Strategy, in career planning, 141–44
Summit Consulting Group, 209

T–U

Task forces, 147–48
Taxes
deductions for job-search costs,
162
and severance pay, 158
Teamwork, 75–77, 209–10
collaborative spirit and, 87
and networking, 169
work organization and, 114–15
"Tears and Weeping Among
Professional Women: In Search of
New Understanding," 202
Technology
continuing education and, 179–80
workforce management and, 87

Temporary jobs, 33, 42
Total Quality Management, 75
Townsend, Larry, 191–92
U.S. Department of Labor's Bureau
    of Labor Statistics, 80
Uchitelle, Louis, 113
Unemployment compensation, 158,
    162–63

V
Vacation days, 137
Values, 213
Vested self-interest, 168. *See also*
    Networking
Video resumes, 28, 22
Volunteer work, 10, 24, 29, 148, 212
    as preparation for new career,
        224
    within company, 147–48

W
Will-Burt Company, 185
Window views, in office, 193
Women
    and discrimination, 45, 51, 118,
        150
    as managers, 91–92
    needs and desires in
        workplace, 94
    and networking, 169–70
Women's Networks, 170
Workers' compensation, 30
Workers in transition, 159
Workforce
    changes in, 45, 74–75, 80–81
    diversity in, 46
Working abroad, 31–32
Workshops, 137, 150
Wrongful discharge, 157